THINK
AND
GROW RICH
...IN A MINUTE

Edited by Bill Hartley and Ann Hartley

with commentary by Bill Hartley

HIGHROADS MEDIA, INC.

ISBN-10: 1-932429-61-1
ISBN-13: 978-1-932429-61-9
10 9 8 7 6 5 4 3 2 1

Contents

Chapter I

What You Need to Know Before You Get Started

Think and Grow Rich . . . In a Minute is the perfect book for you to have in your own library, and it is an equally perfect book for you to give as a gift to someone you want to inspire, encourage, or motivate.

This is the ideal book for anyone who hasn't yet read *Think and Grow Rich* but who wants to get a fast take on what makes it the best-selling success book ever published.

And it is just as appropriate for those who are already familiar with Napoleon Hill's Principles of Success but who would welcome a way to zero in on the key concepts to recapture those "aha!" moments that got them feeling so motivated the first time around.

This edition of *Think and Grow Rich* is designed specifically to highlight only the A material. It is the refined version, narrowed down and focused on just the best of the best. And although not every single item can be read in exactly sixty seconds or less, *Think and Grow Rich…In a Minute* does get right to the very heart of Napoleon Hill's key ideas in the quickest and most direct way.

In preparing this edition, the editors carefully went through the original bestseller to identify the key concept underlying each chapter, then reexamined the material to find the very best of Hill's observations, advice, anecdotes, and maxims that most clearly and concisely explained the main principle of success for each chapter.

The resulting book follows the format of the original, but refines the central message of each chapter into a collection of short, sharp, to-the-point stories and commentaries that are quick to read and easy to understand—while still conveying the essence of Napoleon Hill's philosophy of personal achievement.

$$\text{s s \$ ⧖ ¢ ¢ ¢}$$

Woven throughout the chapters of the original *Think and Grow Rich* are certain basic concepts that are the foundation of Napoleon Hill's Principles of Success. Readers of the full-length book gradually learn those basic concepts as they advance through the chapters, but because of the format of this focused edition, it will be most helpful to readers to have those basics explained here in the introduction.

THE CARNEGIE SECRET—OR THE LAW OF ATTRACTION

The Carnegie secret is a variation on the Law of Attraction or the power of positive thinking, which says that if you hold a particular desire in your mind, and you focus positive thoughts on that desire, the thing that you desire in your mind will be attracted to you in reality.

Andrew Carnegie and Napoleon Hill had a slightly different take on this concept. They did not believe that visualizing your desire could "manifest" things and put actual dollars in your bank, or park a Rolls-Royce in your driveway, any more than it could make a cup and saucer suddenly materialize on the desk in front of you.

Thinking positively and visualizing things the way you want them to be doesn't create concrete objects; it creates attitudes and ideas. When you change your attitudes and ideas, you naturally go from thinking about what you desire, to thinking about how to get what you desire, to actually making things happen in the real world to *achieve* your desire.

INFINITE INTELLIGENCE

Infinite Intelligence is the term that Hill created to describe the matrix of connections that your mind taps into when it comes up with flashes of insight, intuitions, off-the-wall hunches, and inspired solutions.

Most of the creative ideas you come up with that appear in your imagination are made up from bits and pieces of information that is stored in your subconscious mind. But sometimes you will have an idea or a solution to a problem that seems to come to you from "out of the blue." These kinds of ideas "feel" different—like you don't know how or where the information came from that they are made up of. You call them hunches, intuitions, or inspirations.

Hill says that the bursts of electrical energy generated when thoughts or ideas are created in your mind are similar to radio waves, and like radio waves, they radiate outward from the source.

Most times these thought waves are at such a low level that they are not noticeable. But occasionally the frequency of vibration of one of these waves of energy will correspond to the frequency of your mind, and the thought wave will appear in your imagination as a hunch or a premonition.

Hill's term *Infinite Intelligence* describes both the ideas that are interconnecting in your subconscious as well as those ideas that come to you in the form of waves of energy.

THE ETHER

Napoleon Hill says that all things in the universe are interconnected, but if all things are connected, then there needs to be something in between the individual things that connects them to each other. Hill calls that connecting stuff the *ether.*

Originally, *ether* was a term that was used by nineteenth-century scientists to explain how light from the stars could travel through the void of space. At that time it was known that light travels in waves, but in space there is no atmosphere to transmit the waves of light.

To overcome this problem, scientists proposed that there must be something else that filled the void and would carry waves of light, and they called this "something else" the ether.

Without getting into an even longer explanation, suffice it to say that Albert Einstein came along and offered theories that made it a nonissue. However, Napoleon Hill continued to use the term "the ether" to describe his concept of the stuff that fills all voids and therefore acts as a connection between all things.

It is a fact that in the universe there are only four things: time, space, mass, and energy. Further, every "thing" is made up of either mass or energy, and mass is actually just energy in a different form. The human body is made up of energy, the human mind is energy, the ether is energy, and the thoughts and ideas that come into the mind are also energy.

Hill says that because everything is connected to everything else in this way, the thoughts you focus on in your mind can have an effect on what happens in the outside world, as when your mind connects with outside thoughts that appear in your imagination as hunches or premonitions.

THE MASTER MIND ALLIANCE

A Master Mind is formed when two or more people come together to focus on the same problem to find a solution, and it is the combination of their minds that attracts the creative ideas to solve the problem.

If humans sometimes pick up external thought waves that appear in the imagination in the form of hunches or intuitions, is it not likely that the members of a group who are chosen specifically because they share the same definite chief aim are even more likely to make such connections?

By definition, the members of a Master Mind are committed to the same philosophy, and with multiple minds focused on the same definite chief aim, all members also share access to a wider, deeper communal pool of Infinite Intelligence. The combination will produce insights and ideas that the individual minds would never have come up with independently.

The theory of the Master Mind is that two heads are not only better than one, they are better than two—because the combination is greater than the sum of its parts. No two minds ever come together without creating this third invisible, intangible force which, in the case of a Master Mind, will produce insights and ideas that neither of the individual minds would have come up with independently.

ABOUT THE EDITING THEORY

As you read further into this book you will find that variations on the explanations of the four basic concepts will be repeated in a number of different chapters. This repetition is due to another of Hill's basic concepts: that an idea needs to be repeated over and over in order for it to become embedded in the subconscious.

As the excerpts from the original edition of *Think and Grow Rich* were being assembled into the chapters of this new edition, the editors approached the written text as we would that of a living author. When we encountered what modern grammarians would consider to be run-on sentences, outdated punctuation, or other matters of form, we opted for contemporary usage.

Some editing has been done to bring related sections of text into closer proximity to one another, but in every case the original context has been preserved and the original meaning remains unchanged. In a few instances, alterations have been made to correct scientific information that has since become outdated.

All editorial commentary is clearly set off in the same sans serif font in which the words you are now reading are typeset. All original text excerpted from *Think and Grow Rich* appears in a serif font, which is easily distinguishable from the editor's commentary.

ABOUT THE EDITORS

For more than twenty years, the publisher/editors of this book, Bill Hartley and Ann Hartley, have not only been deeply involved in the study of Napoleon Hill's writings, but have also been the leading publishers of his works. As publishers, producers, and editors, they have created and published more bestselling books and audiobooks by and about Napoleon Hill than any other publisher in the world.

Chapter 2

Napoleon Hill Explains
The Carnegie Secret

The following is excerpted from the opening paragraphs written by Napoleon Hill for the Author's Preface to *Think and Grow Rich*:

In every chapter of this book, mention has been made of the money-making secret that has made fortunes for more than five hundred exceedingly wealthy men whom I have carefully analyzed over a long period of years.

The secret was brought to my attention by Andrew Carnegie more than a quarter of a century ago. When he saw that I had grasped the idea, he asked if I would be willing to spend twenty years or more, preparing myself to take it to the world, to men and women who, without the secret, might go through life as failures. I said I would, and with Mr. Carnegie's cooperation, I have kept my promise.

$$ssS\$ \$ \$ss$$

Napoleon Hill learned the Carnegie secret when he was working as a writer for a magazine and was assigned to write a profile of the famed steel baron and philanthropist. Hill had been granted three hours in which to interview him. However, by the end of the allotted time, Carnegie had become so taken with the intelligence of this intense young interviewer that he kept extending their meeting until it had stretched into a three-day marathon. *Think and Grow Rich* is a direct result of what Hill learned at that meeting.

$$ssS\$ \$ \$ss$$

Mr. Carnegie believed the formula should be taught in all public schools and colleges, and expressed the opinion that if it were properly taught it would so revolutionize the entire educational system that the time spent in school could be reduced to less than half.

$$ssS\$ \$ \$ss$$

While I was performing the twenty-year task of research, which I had undertaken at Mr. Carnegie's request, I analyzed hundreds of well-known men who had accumulated their vast fortunes through the aid of the Carnegie secret.

To illustrate the point, in the original book Hill lists forty-seven of the most successful and wealthy men in America, including famous industrialists, entrepreneurs, inventors, businessmen, and leaders of every sort including two presidents of the United States.

These names represent but a small fraction of the hundreds of well-known Americans whose achievements—financially and otherwise—prove that those who understand and apply the Carnegie secret reach high stations in life.

- I have never known anyone who was inspired to use the secret who did not achieve noteworthy success in their chosen calling.

- I have never known any person to distinguish themself, or to accumulate riches of any consequence, without possession of the secret.

From these two facts I draw the conclusion that this secret is very important as part of the knowledge essential for self-determination—more than any that one receives through what is popularly known as "education."

THE CARNEGIE SECRET

The secret to which I refer has been mentioned no fewer than a hundred times throughout this book [the original edition]. It has not been directly named, for it seems to work more successfully when it is merely uncovered and left in sight, where those who are ready, and searching for it, may pick it up.

Education has nothing to do with it. Long before I was born the secret had found its way into the possession of Thomas A. Edison, and he used it so intelligently that he became the world's leading inventor, although he had but three months of schooling.

I am not attempting to minimize the value of schooling, but I am trying to express my earnest belief that those who master and apply the secret will reach high stations, accumulate riches, and bargain with life on their own terms, even if their schooling has been meager.

The secret cannot be had without a price, although the price is far less than its value.

It cannot be had at any price by those who are not intentionally searching for it.

It cannot be given away, it cannot be purchased for money, for the reason that it comes in two parts. One part is already in the possession of those who are ready for it.

As a final word of preparation before you begin the next chapter, may I offer one brief suggestion which may provide a clue by which the Carnegie secret may be recognized? It is this . . .

ALL ACHIEVEMENT, ALL EARNED RICHES, HAVE THEIR BEGINNING IN AN IDEA!

If you are ready for the secret, you already possess one-half of it. Therefore, you will readily recognize the other half the moment it reaches your mind.

Chapter 3

INTRODUCTION:
The Man Who Thought His Way into Partnership with Thomas A. Edison

To open the first chapter of *Think and Grow Rich,* Napoleon Hill tells the story of Edwin C. Barnes to illustrate the importance of knowing clearly what you want and committing yourself to your goal.

Barnes was the only man who ever became a partner of famed inventor Thomas Alva Edison. However, when he set that goal for himself he had never met Edison, he knew nothing about inventing, and he was so broke he did not have enough money for a train ticket to Orange, New Jersey, where Edison had his laboratory. But Barnes was so certain of his desire that he hopped a freight train and rode all the way in an empty boxcar, then he walked to the laboratory and announced that he was there to go into business with Edison.

ss$$ $$ss

Speaking of the first meeting between Barnes and Edison, years later, Mr. Edison said, "He stood there before me looking like an ordinary tramp, but there was something in the expression of his face which conveyed the impression that he was determined to get what he had come after.

"I had learned, from years of experience with men, that when a man really desires a thing so deeply that he is willing to stake his whole future on a single turn of the wheel in order to get it, he is sure to win.

"I gave him the opportunity he asked for, because I saw he had made up his mind to stand by until he succeeded. Subsequent events proved that no mistake was made."

Just what young Barnes said to Mr. Edison on that occasion was far less important than what he *thought*.

Truly, "thoughts are things," and powerful things at that, when they are mixed with definiteness of purpose, persistence, and a burning desire for their translation into riches, or other material objects.

If the significance of this statement could be conveyed to every person who reads it, there would be no need for the remainder of this book.

ss$$ $$ss

One of the chief characteristics of Barnes' desire was that it was definite. He wanted to work *with* Edison, not *for* him.

Barnes did not say to himself, "Aw well, what's the use? I guess I'll change my mind and try for a salesman's job." But he did say, "I came here to go into business with Edison, and I'll accomplish this end if it takes the remainder of my life." He meant it.

What a different story people would have to tell if only they would adopt a definite purpose and stand by that purpose until it had time to become an all-consuming obsession.

Thomas Edison had just perfected a new office device, known at that time as the Edison Dictating Machine. His salesmen were not enthusiastic over the machine.

Barnes knew he could sell the Edison Dictating Machine. He suggested this to Edison and promptly got his chance. In fact he sold it so successfully that Edison gave him a contract to distribute and market it all over the nation.

Out of that business association grew the slogan "Made by Edison and installed by Barnes."

Barnes literally thought himself into a partnership with the great Edison! He thought himself into a fortune. He had nothing to start with except the capacity to know what he wanted and the determination to stand by that desire until he realized it.

He had no money to begin with. He had but little education. He had no influence. But he did have initiative, faith, and the will to win. With these intangible forces he made himself the number-one man with the greatest inventor who ever lived.

When the opportunity came, it appeared in a different form and from a different direction than Barnes had expected. That is one of the tricks of opportunity. It has a sly habit of slipping in by the back door, and often it comes disguised in the form of misfortune or temporary defeat.

Perhaps this is why so many fail to recognize opportunity.

$ $ $$ $ $

THREE FEET FROM GOLD

To further emphasize the importance of staying with your plan until you succeed, Hill tells how his friend R. U. Darby and his uncle joined the gold rush, went out west, and within a few months struck a vein.

The first car of ore was mined and shipped to a smelter. The returns proved they had one of the richest mines in Colorado!

Down went the drills. Up went the hopes of Darby and Uncle. Then something happened. The vein of gold ore disappeared! They had come to the end of the rainbow and the pot of gold was no longer there. They drilled on, desperately trying to pick up the vein again—all to no avail.

Finally, they quit. They sold the machinery to a junk man for a few hundred dollars and took the train back home.

The junk man called in a mining engineer to look at the mine and do a little calculating. The engineer advised that the project had failed because the owners were not familiar with "fault lines." His calculations showed that the vein would be found just three feet from where the Darbys had stopped drilling! That is exactly where it was found.

The "junk" man took millions of dollars in ore from the mine, because he knew enough to seek expert counsel before giving up.

"That experience was a blessing in disguise. It taught me to keep on keeping on, no matter how hard the going may be—a lesson I needed to learn before I could succeed in anything."

And learn his lesson he did. R. U. Darby became one of America's most successful insurance salesmen, and he always maintained that part of his success came from repeating to himself his new motto:

"I stopped three feet from gold, but I will never stop because men say no when I ask them to buy insurance."

$ $ $$ $$ $ $

One of the most common causes of failure is the habit of quitting when one is overtaken by temporary defeat.

$ $ $$ $$ $ $

∾ $ ல

JUST BECAUSE YOU THINK SO,
THAT DOESN'T MAKE IT RIGHT

Another weakness found in altogether too many people is the habit of measuring everything and everyone by their own impressions and beliefs. Some who will read this will believe that no one can think and grow rich. They cannot think in terms of riches because their thought habits have been steeped in poverty, want, misery, failure, and defeat.

These unfortunate people remind me of a prominent Chinese gentleman who came to America to be educated in American ways. He attended the University of Chicago. One day President Harper met this young man on the campus, stopped to chat with him for a few minutes, and asked what had impressed him as being the most noticeable characteristic of the American people.

"Why," the man exclaimed, "the slant of your eyes!"

We refuse to believe that which we do not understand. We foolishly believe that our own limitations are the *proper* measure of limitations. Sure, the other fellow's eyes are "off slant," BECAUSE THEY ARE NOT THE SAME AS OUR OWN.

ல $ ∾

INVICTUS

Out of the night that covers me,
Black as the Pit from pole to pole,
I thank whatever gods may be
For my unconquerable soul.

In the fell clutch of circumstance
I have not winced nor cried aloud;
Under the bludgeonings of chance
My head is bloody, but unbowed.

Beyond this place of wrath and tears
Looms but the Horror of the shade,
And yet the menace of the years
Finds and shall find me unafraid.

It matters not how strait the gate,
How charged with punishments the scroll;
I am the master of my fate,
I am the captain of my soul.

—WILLIAM ERNEST HENLEY

YOU ARE THE MASTER OF YOUR FATE, THE CAPTAIN OF YOUR SOUL, BECAUSE . . .

When Henley wrote the prophetic lines, "I am the master of my fate, I am the captain of my soul," he should have informed us that we are the masters of our fate, the captains of our souls, because we have the power to control our thoughts.

He should have told us, with great emphasis, that this power makes no attempt to discriminate between destructive thoughts and constructive thoughts; that it will urge us to translate into physical reality thoughts of poverty, just as quickly as it will influence us to act upon thoughts of riches.

He should have told us, too, that our brains become magnetized with the dominating thoughts that we hold in our minds, and these "magnets" attract to us the forces, the people, the circumstances of life which harmonize with the nature of our dominating thoughts.

He could have told us that before we can accumulate riches in great abundance, we must magnetize our minds with intense desire for riches, that we must become "money conscious until the desire for money drives us to definite plans for acquiring it."

But being a poet and not a philosopher, Henley contented himself by stating a great truth in poetic form, leaving those who followed to interpret the philosophical meaning of his lines.

∽ $ ᫤

Chapter 4

DESIRE:
The Starting Point of All Achievement

The First Step Toward Riches

Napoleon Hill makes it clear that when your desire is to accomplish a specific objective, and you want to use his philosophy of personal achievement to accomplish that desire, you must begin by knowing precisely what you desire and you must be able to visualize your desired goal so clearly that you can hold the image in your mind.

Napoleon Hill refers to this kind of desire as having a *definite chief aim,* and when you have a definite chief aim it is much more than wishing or dreaming for something, and it is more demanding than what other success systems often term goal-seeking.

When you have a desire or definite chief aim as Hill defines it, every single action you take boils down to one question: Will doing this help me achieve my desire, or won't it?

WHEN FORWARD IS THE ONLY WAY TO GO

A long while ago, a great warrior faced a situation that made it necessary for him to make a decision which ensured his success on the battlefield. He was about to send his armies against a powerful foe whose men outnumbered his own.

He loaded his soldiers onto boats, sailed to the enemy's country, unloaded soldiers and equipment, then gave the order to burn the ships that had carried them.

Addressing his men before the first battle, he said, "You see the boats going up in smoke. This means that we cannot leave these shores alive unless we win! We now have no choice—we win, or we perish!

They won.

TURNING BACK SHOULDN'T ENTER YOUR MIND

When Edwin C. Barnes climbed down from the freight train in Orange, New Jersey, he may have resembled a tramp, but his thoughts were those of a king!

Barnes' desire was not a hope. It was not a wish. It was a pulsating desire which transcended all else. It was definite.

Barnes succeeded because he chose a definite goal, placed all his energy, all his willpower, all his effort, everything behind that goal. He did not become the partner of Edison the day he arrived. He was content to start in the most menial work, as long as it provided an opportunity to take even one step toward his cherished goal.

To everyone, except himself, he appeared only another cog in the Edison business wheel. But in Edwin Barnes' own mind, he was the partner of Edison every minute of the time, from the very day that he first went to work there.

It is a remarkable illustration of the power of a definite desire. Barnes won his goal because he wanted to be a business associate of Mr. Edison's more than he wanted anything else. He created a plan by which to attain that purpose, but he burned all bridges behind him. He stood by his desire until it became the dominating obsession of his life—and, finally, a fact.

When he went to Orange, he did not say to himself, "I will try to induce Edison to give me a job of some sort." He did not say, "I will work there for a few months, and if I get no encouragement I will quit and get a job somewhere else."

He said, "There is but one thing in this world that I am determined to have, and that is a business association with Thomas A. Edison. I will burn all bridges behind me, and stake my entire future on my ability to get what I want."

He left himself no possible way of retreat. He had to win, or perish. That is all there is to the Barnes story of success!

ss$$$$zzzz

Every person who wins in any undertaking must be willing to burn their ships and cut all sources of retreat. Only by so doing can you be sure of maintaining that state of mind known as a burning desire to win. It is essential to success.

ss$$$$zzzz

Remember, no more effort is required to aim high in life, to demand abundance and prosperity, than is required to accept misery and poverty.

ss$$$$zzzz

Only those who become "money conscious" can ever accumulate great riches. "Money consciousness" means that the mind has become so thoroughly saturated with the desire for money that you can see yourself already in possession of it.

ss$$$$zzzz

Every human being who reaches the age of understanding of the purpose of money, wishes for it. Wishing will not bring riches. But desiring riches with a state of mind that becomes an obsession, then planning definite ways to acquire riches, and backing those plans with persistence which does not recognize failure, will bring riches.

ss$$$$zzzz

SIX STEPS TO TURN YOUR DESIRE INTO MONEY

1. Fix in your mind the exact amount of money you desire. It is not sufficient merely to say "I want plenty of money." Be definite as to the amount.

2. Determine exactly what you intend to give in return for the money you desire. (There is no such reality as "something for nothing.")

3. Establish a definite date when you intend to possess the money you desire.

4. Create a definite plan for carrying out your desire, and begin at once—whether you are ready or not—to put this plan into action.

5. Write out a clear, concise statement of the amount of money you intend to acquire, name the time frame for its acquisition, state what you intend to give in return for the money, and describe clearly the plan through which you intend to accumulate it.

6. Read your written statement aloud, twice daily—once just before retiring at night and once after arising in the morning. As you read, see and feel and believe yourself already in possession of the money.

$ $ $ $ $ $

If you do not see great riches in your imagination, you will never see them in your bank balance.

$ $ $ $ $ $

You may complain that it is impossible for you to "see yourself in possession of money" before you actually have it. Here is where a burning desire will come to your aid.

If you truly desire money so keenly that your desire is an obsession, you will have no difficulty in convincing yourself that you will acquire it.

The object is to want money and to become so determined to have it that you convince yourself you will have it.

You may as well know, right here, that you can never have riches in great quantities, unless you can work yourself into a white heat of desire for money, and actually believe you will possess it.

DREAMS ARE THE SEEDLINGS OF REALITY

We who desire to accumulate riches should remember that the real leaders of the world always have been men who harnessed, and put into practical use, the intangible unseen forces of unborn opportunity, and have converted those forces (or impulses of thought) into skyscrapers, cities, factories, airplanes, automobiles, and every form of convenience that makes life more pleasant.

Henry Ford, poor and uneducated, dreamed of a horse-less carriage, went to work with what tools he possessed without waiting for opportunity to favor him, and now evidence of his dream belts the entire earth. He has put more wheels into operation than any man who ever lived, because he was not afraid to back his dreams.

Thomas Edison dreamed of a lamp that could be operated by electricity, began where he stood to put his dream into action, and despite more than ten thousand failures, he stood by that dream until he made it a physical reality.

Practical dreamers do not quit!

NO ONE IS EVER DEFEATED
UNTIL DEFEAT HAS BEEN ACCEPTED
AS A REALITY!

Napoleon Hill closes this chapter with a story which makes it very clear that he had personal experience with the power that comes from an unwavering focus on a definite chief aim or desire. It is the story of how Hill taught his son Blair to use his mind to overcome the challenge of being born not only deaf but also without ears or any other way for sound waves to travel to his brain.

At that time Hill was already deeply immersed in the principles that underlie his philosophy of personal achievement, and he became determined that by applying the principles of his philosophy he would find a way to help his son overcome his handicap. The first glimmer of hope came when he saw that his little boy loved to clamp his teeth on the edge of the Victrola so that he could feel the sound vibrations. Hill then discovered that Blair would react when he spoke to him with his lips touching Blair's mastoid bone at the base of the brain.

Having determined that he could hear the sound of my voice plainly, I began immediately to transfer to his mind the desire to hear and speak. I soon discovered that the child enjoyed bedtime stories, so I went to work creating stories designed to develop in him self-reliance, imagination, and a keen desire to hear and to be normal.

There was one story in particular, which I emphasized by giving it some new and dramatic coloring each time it was told. It was designed to plant in his mind the thought that his affliction was not a liability but an asset of great value; that every adversity brings with it the seed of an equivalent advantage.

From that point onward, Blair was raised like any other boy. He did not go to a special school, nor did he learn sign language. With his father and mother's encouragement, he learned to cope with his handicap in his own way. He was a gifted student through school and university, but it wasn't until he had graduated university that he finally found an electronic device that could actually help him overcome his unique condition and hear for the first time. He immediately contacted the company that manufactured the device and sold them on the idea that he was the perfect person to market their hearing aid for them.

There is no doubt in my mind that Blair would have been a deaf mute all his life, if his mother and I had not managed to shape his mind as we did.

I planted in my son's mind the desire to hear and speak as any normal person hears and speaks. That desire has now become a reality. I planted in his mind the desire to convert his greatest handicap into his greatest asset. That desire has been realized.

The modus operandi by which this astounding result was achieved is not hard to describe. It consisted of three very definite facts:

1. I mixed faith with the desire for normal hearing, which I passed on to my son.

2. I communicated my desire to him in every conceivable way available, through persistent, continuous effort, over a period of years.

3. HE BELIEVED ME.

I believe in the power of desire backed by faith, because I have seen this power lift people from lowly beginnings to places of power and wealth.

I have seen it rob the grave of its victims; I have seen it serve as the medium by which people staged a comeback after having been defeated in a hundred different ways.

I have seen it provide my own son with a normal, happy, successful life, despite nature's having sent him into the world without ears.

Through some strange and powerful principle of "mental chemistry," which she has never divulged, nature wraps up in the impulse of strong desire "that something" which recognizes no such word as *impossible* and accepts no such reality as failure.

Truly, my own son has taught me that handicaps can be converted into steppingstones on which one may climb toward some worthy goal, unless they are accepted as obstacles and used as alibis.

ssS$ZZzz

SUCCESS REQUIRES NO APOLOGIES, FAILURE PERMITS NO ALIBIS.

ssS$ZZzz

Chapter 5

FAITH:

Visualization of and Belief in Attainment of Desire

The Second Step Toward Riches

In modern usage, the word *faith* has become almost interchangeable with religious belief, but that is not the way Napoleon Hill uses the word in *Think and Grow Rich*. Faith, as it is used here, means having confidence, trust, and an absolute unwavering belief that you can accomplish your desire or goal.

In this chapter Hill focuses on two key aspects of faith.

First, that you can create faith within yourself by intentionally planting belief and self-confidence in your subconscious mind.

Second, that when you have created within yourself the faith that you can achieve your desire, just having that faith in your ability will cause more creative ideas and solutions to come to your mind.

CREATING FAITH THROUGH AUTOSUGGESTION

Faith is a state of mind which may be induced, or created, by affirmation or repeated instructions to the subconscious mind, through the principle of autosuggestion.

Repetition of affirmations (or orders to your subconscious mind) is the only known method of voluntary development of the emotion of faith.

You may convince your subconscious mind that you believe you will receive what you ask for, and it will act upon that belief which your subconscious mind passes back to you in the form of faith.

Your belief, or faith, is the element that determines the action of your subconscious mind. There is nothing to hinder you from "deceiving" your subconscious mind when giving it instructions through autosuggestion, as I deceived my son's subconscious mind.

To make this "deceit" more realistic, conduct yourself just as you would if you were already in possession of the material thing that you are demanding when you call upon your subconscious mind.

The subconscious mind will transmute into its physical equivalent any order which is given to it in a state of belief, or faith, that the order will be carried out.

AFFIRMATIONS AND VISUALIZATIONS

Faith, self-confidence, and belief in your ability can be intentionally planted in your subconscious mind through the use of positive affirmations and visualizations.

POSITIVE AFFIRMATIONS: These are short phrases that clearly state the changes you want to make in yourself. If you emotionalize such a phrase with total faith and belief that you are capable of changing yourself, and if you repeat the phrase over and over to yourself until thinking that way becomes your natural habit, then you will make the change you desire. It is the repetition that wears away at your old thinking until it makes a new mental pathway.

VISUALIZATIONS: These are the visual equivalent of affirmations. Visualizations are mental movies that you play over and over in your mind, creating such vivid mental images of the change you desire that you experience it just as if it were reality. By making it so real in your mind, you are emotionalizing your desire, and the more emotionalized it is, the deeper it is burned into your subconscious. When you have firmly planted belief in yourself in your subconscious, self-confidence will become your natural reaction.

FAITH AND THE LAW OF ATTRACTION

Any impulse of thought which is repeatedly passed on to the subconscious mind is, finally, accepted and acted upon by the subconscious mind, which proceeds to translate that impulse into its physical equivalent by the most practical procedure available.

Each person is what they are because of the dominating thoughts they permit to occupy their mind.

Thoughts that are mixed with any of the feelings or emotions constitute a "magnetic" force which attracts, from the vibrations of the "ether," other similar or related thoughts.

THE ETHER

The *ether,* as Hill uses the term, is the "medium" through which all things are interconnected. As was explained in chapter 1, What You Need to Know, because all things—including you, your thoughts, the ether, and everything else in creation—are just different forms of energy, everything shares something in common with everything else.

Because of these common bonds or connnections, when you have a thought of a certain kind, it is possible that via the ether your thoughts are picking up some influences from other similar thoughts that are "out there" and also a part of the common pool or ether.

The human mind is constantly attracting vibrations which harmonize with that which dominates the human mind. Any thought, idea, plan, or purpose that one holds in one's mind attracts, from the vibrations of the ether, a host of its relatives. It then grows until it becomes the dominating master of the individual in whose mind it has been housed.

Faith is the head chemist of the mind. When faith is blended with the vibrations of thought, the subconscious mind instantly picks up the vibration, translates it into its spiritual equivalent, and transmits it to Infinite Intelligence.

INFINITE INTELLIGENCE

The ether is the medium that interconnects all things, and Infinite Intelligence is the matrix it connects you with.

Infinite Intelligence is the part of the human thinking process that pulls together bits and pieces of ideas hidden in your subconscious and turns them into ideas that then flash into your imagination as hunches or inspirations.

Infinite Intelligence is also that part of your mind which sometimes works in a way similar to an antenna picking up stray radio waves. But your mind does it with outside thought waves that occasionally hit the right frequency and suddenly show up in your mind as hunches, intuitions, or premonitions about things outside your field of knowledge.

BOTH POVERTY AND RICHES
ARE THE OFFSPRING OF THOUGHT

All riches and all material things that anyone acquires through self-effort begin in the form of a clear, concise mental picture of the thing one seeks. When that picture grows to the proportions of an obsession, it is taken over by the subconscious mind. From that point on, you are attracted in the direction of the physical equivalent of the mental picture.

The subconscious mind may be likened to a magnet. When it has been thoroughly saturated with any definite purpose, it has a decided tendency to attract all that is necessary for the fulfillment of that purpose.

Napoleon Hill's philosophy agrees in principle with this concept, which is often called the Law of Attraction or the Power of Positive Thinking. However, as noted in chapter 1, Hill does not believe that visualizing your desire can put actual dollars in your bank, or park a Rolls-Royce in your driveway, any more than it can make a cup and saucer suddenly materialize on the desk in front of you.

Hill says that when you focus your mind on what you desire, what it attracts are the ideas and plans that you can use to *achieve* your desire—not the actual dollar bills, automobiles, or crockery.

When you visualize yourself acquiring money, a car, or any other real object, what you are really doing is confirming to yourself the belief that achieving what you desire is a possibility, and that you are a person who is capable of making it happen.

The vivid images that you create of your desire are burned into your subconscious, where they connect and interact with other bits of information, so that your mind automatically starts coming up with more and better ideas of how you can earn the money to put in your bank account so you can buy the Rolls-Royce.

Thinking positively and visualizing things the way you want them to be doesn't create concrete objects; it creates attitudes and ideas. When you change your attitudes and ideas, you naturally go from thinking about what you desire, to thinking about how to get what you desire, to actually making things happen in the real world to achieve your desire.

That is how positive thinking turns into positive results: Thinking prompts you to act, and it is your actions that make the concrete things come true.

∽ $ ∽

> If you fill your mind with fear, doubt, and unbelief in your ability to connect with and use the forces of Infinite Intelligence, the law of autosuggestion will take this spirit of unbelief and use it as a pattern by which your subconscious mind will translate it into its physical equivalent: fear and doubt in your ability.

WATCH WHAT YOU THINK—EVEN TO YOURSELF

You may develop faith by voluntarily suggesting to your subconscious mind that you have faith. The mind comes, finally, to take on the nature of the influences which dominate it.

Understand this truth and you will know why it is essential for you to encourage the positive emotions as dominating forces of your mind, and discourage and eliminate negative emotions.

The subconscious mind makes no distinction between constructive and destructive thought impulses. It works with the material we feed it through our thoughts.

The subconscious mind will translate, into its physical equivalent, a thought impulse of a negative or destructive nature just as readily as it will act upon thought impulses of a positive or constructive nature. This accounts for what is referred to as misfortune or bad luck.

There are millions of people who believe themselves "doomed" to poverty and failure because of some strange force over which they believe they have no control. They are the creators of their own "misfortunes," because of this negative belief that is picked up by the subconscious mind and translated into its physical equivalent.

Those who go down in defeat and distress do so because of negative application of the principle of autosuggestion.

THINKING

If you think you are beaten, you are;
If you think you dare not, you don't.
If you like to win but you think you can't,
It is almost certain you won't.

If you think you'll lose, you've lost,
For out of the world we find
Success begins with a fellow's will;
It's all in the state of mind.

If you think you are outclassed, you are;
You've got to think high to rise.
You've got to be sure of yourself before
You can ever win a prize.

Life's battles don't always go
To the stronger or faster man;
But soon or late the man who wins
Is the one WHO THINKS HE CAN.

—WALTER D. WINTLE

SELF-CONFIDENCE THROUGH AUTOSUGGESTION

Napoleon Hill says that to some degree we all suffer from lack of self-confidence. This handicap can be overcome through autosuggestion: positive thoughts stated in writing, memorized, and repeated until they become a part of your subconscious mind.

THE SELF-CONFIDENCE FORMULA

First. I know that I have the ability to achieve the object of my Definite Purpose in life. Therefore, I demand of myself persistent, continuous action toward its attainment, and I here and now promise to render such action.

Second. I realize that the dominating thoughts of my mind will eventually reproduce themselves in outward, physical action and gradually transform themselves into physical reality. Therefore, I will concentrate my thoughts for thirty minutes daily on the task of thinking of the person I intend to become, thereby creating in my mind a clear mental picture of that person.

Third. I know, through the principle of autosuggestion, that any desire I persistently hold in my mind will eventually seek expression through some practical means of attaining the object behind it. Therefore, I will devote ten minutes daily to demanding of myself the development of self-confidence.

Fourth. I have clearly written down a description of my definite chief aim in life, and I will never stop trying until I shall have developed sufficient self-confidence for its attainment.

Fifth. I fully realize that no wealth or position can long endure unless built upon truth and justice. Therefore, I will engage in no transaction which does not benefit all whom it affects.

- I will succeed by attracting to myself the forces I wish to use and the cooperation of other people.

- I will induce others to serve me, because of my willingness to serve others.

- I will eliminate hatred, envy, jealousy, selfishness, and cynicism by developing love for all humanity, because I know that a negative attitude toward others can never bring me success.

- I will cause others to believe in me, because I will believe in them and in myself.

Sixth. I will sign my name to this formula, commit it to memory, and repeat it aloud once a day, with full faith that it will gradually influence my thoughts and actions so that I will become a self-reliant and successful person.

ss$$S$ss

Now, let us go back to the starting point as to how the original seed of an idea, plan, or purpose may be planted in the mind:

- Any idea, plan, or purpose may be placed in the mind through repetition of thought.

- This is why you are asked to write out a statement of your major purpose, or definite chief aim, commit it to memory, and repeat it in audible words, day after day, until these vibrations of sound have reached your subconscious mind.

- We are what we are because of the vibrations of thought that we pick up and register through the stimuli of our daily environment.

ss$$S$ss

Chapter 6

AUTOSUGGESTION:
The Medium for Influencing the Subconscious Mind

The Third Step Toward Riches

Autosuggestion is a term which applies to all suggestions and all self-administered stimuli that reach one's mind through the five senses. Stated in another way, autosuggestion is self-suggestion.

It is the agency of communication between that part of the mind where conscious thought takes place, and that part which serves as the seat of action for the subconscious mind.

Through the dominating thoughts that you permit to remain in your conscious mind, the principle of autosuggestion voluntarily reaches the subconscious mind and influences it with these thoughts.

AUTOSUGGESTION CAN WORK FOR YOU OR AGAINST YOU

You have learned that any idea you firmly fix in your subconscious mind, by repeated affirmation, automatically becomes a plan or blueprint that an unseen power uses in directing your efforts toward the attainment of the objective in the plan.

If you fill your mind with doubt and unbelief in your ability to achieve, then the principle of autosuggestion takes this spirit of unbelief and sets it up in your subconscious mind as your dominating thought, and slowly but surely it draws you into the whirlpool of *failure.*

But if you fill your mind with radiant self-confidence, the principle of autosuggestion takes *this* belief and sets it up as your dominating thought and helps you master the obstacles that fall in your way until you reach the mountaintop of success.

> # THERE IS ONLY ONE THING IN THE ENTIRE WORLD OVER WHICH YOU HAVE COMPLETE CONTROL . . . AND THAT IS YOUR MIND.

Nature has so built man that he has absolute control over the material that reaches his subconscious mind through his five senses.

Recall what has been said about the subconscious mind resembling a fertile garden spot in which weeds will grow in abundance if the seeds of more desirable crops are not sown therein.

Autosuggestion is the agency of control through which an individual may voluntarily feed their subconscious mind on thoughts of a creative nature, or, by neglect, permit thoughts of a destructive nature to find their way into this rich garden of the mind.

No thought, whether it be negative or positive, can enter the subconscious mind without the aid of the principle of autosuggestion.

Stated differently, all sense impressions which are perceived through the five senses are stopped by the conscious thinking mind and may be either passed on to the subconscious mind or rejected, at will. The conscious mind serves, therefore, as an outerguard to the approach of the subconscious.

HOW TO USE AUTOSUGGESTION
TO VISUALIZE YOUR DEFINITE CHIEF AIM

First. Go to some quiet spot (preferably in bed at night) where you will not be disturbed or interrupted, close your eyes, and repeat aloud (so you may hear your own words) the written statement of the amount of money you intend to accumulate, the time limit for its accumulation, and a description of the service or merchandise you intend to give in return for the money. As you carry out these instructions, see yourself already in possession of the money.

Second. Repeat this program night and morning, until you can see (in your imagination) the money you intend to accumulate.

Third. Place a written copy of your statement where you can see it night and morning, and read it just before retiring and upon arising, until it has been memorized.

WRITING OUT YOUR DEFINITE CHIEF AIM

Suppose that you intend to accumulate $50,000 by the first of January, five years hence, and that you intend to give personal services in return for the money, in the capacity of a salesperson. Your written statement of your purpose should be similar to the following:

- By the first day of January [insert the year] I will have in my possession $50,000, which will come to me in various amounts from time to time during the interim.

- In return for this money I will give the most efficient service of which I am capable, rendering the fullest possible quantity and the best possible quality of service in the capacity of salesperson of [describe the service or merchandise you intend to sell].

- I believe that I will have this money in my possession. My faith is so strong that I can now see this money before my eyes. I can touch it with my hands. It is now awaiting transfer to me at the time, and in the proportion, that I deliver the service I intend to render in return for it.

- I am awaiting a plan by which to accumulate this money, and I will follow that plan when it is received.

IT'S JUST WORDS UNLESS YOU REALLY FEEL IT

When reading aloud the statement of your desire (through which you are endeavoring to develop a "money consciousness"), the mere reading of the words is of no consequence—unless you mix emotion or feeling with your words.

If you repeat a million times the famous formula "Day by day, in every way, I am getting better and better," without mixing emotion and faith with your words, you will experience no desirable results.

Your subconscious mind recognizes and acts upon only thoughts that have been well-mixed with emotion. Plain, unemotional words do not influence the subconscious mind.

Your ability to use the principle of autosuggestion will depend very largely on your capacity to concentrate on a given desire until that desire becomes a burning obsession.

> Man may become the master of himself and of his environment because he has the power to influence his own subconscious mind, and through it gain the cooperation of Infinite Intelligence.

THE SUBCONSCIOUS MIND CANNOT TELL THE DIFFERENCE BETWEEN WHAT IS REAL AND WHAT IS VIVIDLY IMAGINED

Here is a most significant fact: The subconscious mind takes any orders given to it in a spirit of absolute faith, and acts upon those orders.

Following the preceding statement, consider the possibility of playing a perfectly legitimate "trick" on your subconscious mind by making it believe, because you believe it, that:

- you must have the amount of money you are visualizing
- this money is already awaiting your claim
- the subconscious mind must hand over to you practical plans for acquiring the money that is yours.

When visualizing the money you intend to accumulate, see yourself rendering the service or delivering the merchandise you intend to give in return for this money.

Do not wait for a definite plan through which you intend to exchange services or merchandise in return for the money you are visualizing, but begin at once to see yourself in possession of the money, demanding and expecting meanwhile that your subconscious mind will hand over the plan or plans you need.

Be on the alert for these plans and, when they appear, put them into action immediately. When the plans appear, they will probably "flash" into your mind through the sixth sense in the form of an "inspiration."

This inspiration may be considered a direct "telegram" or message from Infinite Intelligence. Treat it with respect and act upon it as soon as you receive it. Failure to do this will be fatal to your success.

ss$$ 22ss

Remember what was said about flashes of inspiration and Infinite Intelligence in the preceding chapters: Because all things share a common connection, when you concentrate all of your attention on a particular desire, idea, or plan, you will attract to yourself other thoughts or ideas that are similar or related to the thought you are focused on.

Sometimes these flashes of insight come out of the forgotten recesses of your subconscious and sometimes they seem to come to you "out of the blue"—hunches or premonitions with no rational reason why you should know the information that makes up the idea.

When these kinds of ideas come to you, it is something more than just coming up with a good idea. This is tapping into Infinite Intelligence, and when these ideas pop into your imagination they have a feel about them that is different than the normal idea.

Infinite Intelligence doesn't always produce ideas on cue, and not all ideas that come to you are brilliant solutions to your desire, but Hill considers these hunches and flashes of insight to be a natural and important part of the thinking process.

They deserve serious consideration, and should be weighed and judged just as you would do with any idea that you arrived at through rational deduction.

THERE ARE NO LIMITATIONS TO THE MIND,
EXCEPT THOSE WE ACKNOWLEDGE.

ssS$$$$ss

Chapter 7

SPECIALIZED KNOWLEDGE:
Personal Experiences
or Observations

The Fourth Step Toward Riches

There are two kinds of knowledge. One is general, the other is specialized. General knowledge, no matter how great in quantity or variety it may be, is of but little use in the accumulation of money.

Knowledge will not attract money, unless it is organized and intelligently directed through practical plans of action. Lack of understanding of this fact has been the source of confusion to millions of people who falsely believe that "knowledge is power." It is nothing of the sort! Knowledge is only potential power. It becomes power only when, and if, it is organized into definite plans of action and directed to a definite end.

EDUCATION, KNOWLEDGE, OR SCHOOLING?

Any person is educated who knows where to get knowledge when they need it, and how to organize that knowledge into definite plans of action.

ss$$ ¢¢¢¢

Thomas A. Edison had only three months of "schooling" during his entire life. He did not lack education, nor did he die poor.

ss$$ ¢¢¢¢

Henry Ford had less than a sixth grade "schooling," but he managed to do pretty well by himself financially. Through the assistance of his Master Mind group, Henry Ford had at his command all the specialized knowledge he needed to enable him to become one of the wealthiest men in America. It was not essential that he have this knowledge in his own mind.

ss$$ ¢¢¢¢

Andrew Carnegie stated that he, personally, knew nothing about the technical end of the steel business; moreover, he did not particularly care to know anything about it. The specialized knowledge that he required for the manufacture and marketing of steel, he found available through the individual units of his Master Mind group.

WHAT IS A MASTER MIND GROUP?

Napoleon Hill defines a Master Mind as follows:

Coordination of knowledge and effort, in a spirit of harmony, between two or more people, for the attainment of a definite purpose. When the minds of two or more people are coordinated in a spirit of harmony, the energy of each mind forms an affinity, and it seems that each mind picks up on the energy of the other minds.

A Master Mind is the result of a conscious attempt by an individual to surround himself or herself with a group of people who are so in-tune with one another that they don't just bring out the best in each other, but the group as a whole takes on a life of its own, elevating everyone's level of thinking, and generating shared leaps of logic, insights, and flashes of intuition.

With multiple minds focused on the same definite chief aim, all members also have access to a wider, deeper, communal pool of Infinite Intelligence. The combination will produce insights and ideas that the individual minds would never have come up with independently.

YOU DON'T HAVE TO HAVE IT YOURSELF
IF YOU KNOW WHERE TO GET IT

People sometimes go through life suffering from "inferiority complexes" because they are not "educated." The person who can organize and direct a Master Mind group of people who possess knowledge useful in the accumulation of money is just as much a person of education as anyone in the group.

Many people make the mistake of assuming that because Henry Ford had but little schooling he is not a man of education. Those who make this mistake do not understand the real meaning of the word "educate." The word is derived from the Latin word "educo," meaning to educe, to draw out, to *develop from within.*

An educated person is not necessarily the one who has an abundance of general or specialized knowledge. An educated person is one who has so developed the faculties of their mind that they may acquire anything they want without violating the rights of others.

The accumulation of great fortunes calls for power, and power is acquired through highly organized and intelligently directed specialized knowledge. But that knowledge does not, necessarily, have to be in the possession of the person who accumulates the fortune.

Anything acquired without effort and without cost is generally unappreciated. Perhaps this is why we get so little from our marvelous opportunity in public schools.

❧ $ ❧

We have in this country what is said to be the greatest public school system in the world, but there is one astounding weakness to this marvelous system—it is free!

One of the strange things about human beings is that they value only that which has a price. The free schools of America, and the free public libraries, do not impress people *because* they are free. This is the major reason why so many people find it necessary to acquire additional training after they quit school and go to work. The person who stops studying merely because they have finished school is forever hopelessly doomed to mediocrity, no matter what may be their calling.

❧ $ ❧

Successful men and women never stop acquiring knowledge. The truth is that schooling does but little more than to put one in the way of learning how to acquire practical knowledge.

❧ $ ❧

Chapter **8**

IMAGINATION:
The Workshop
of the Mind

The Fifth Step Toward Riches

The imagination is literally the workshop wherein are fashioned all plans created by man. The impulse, the desire, is given shape, form, and action through the aid of the imaginative faculty of the mind.

Desire is only a thought, an impulse. It is nebulous and ephemeral. It is abstract, and of no value, until it has been transformed into its physical counterpart.

Ideas are the beginning points of all fortunes. Ideas are products of the imagination.

THERE ARE TWO FORMS OF IMAGINATION

The imaginative faculty functions in two forms. One is known as "synthetic imagination" and the other as "creative imagination."

SYNTHESIZED IMAGINATION

Through this faculty, one may arrange old concepts, ideas, or plans into new combinations. This faculty creates nothing. It merely works with the material of experience, education, and observation with which it is fed. It is the faculty used most by the inventor.

Transformation of the intangible impulse, of desire, into the tangible reality, of money, calls for the use of plans. These plans must be formed with the aid of the imagination and, mainly, with the synthetic faculty.

The most creative people in the world utilize synthesized imagination most of the time to come up with their best ideas. Your synthesized imagination is what you are using when you rack your brain and call upon everything you know to come up with an idea or a solution to a problem. Synthesizing, or putting the right things together in the right way, is the height of creativity. That's what scientists, cooks, inventors, mechanics, songwriters, salespeople, students, business managers, entrepreneurs and just about everyone else does when they are using their head and working to the best of their ability. Using synthesized imagination, you can become hugely successful just by taking the most common everyday thing and seeing how to put it together in a new way.

CREATIVE IMAGINATION

Through the faculty of creative imagination, the finite mind of man has direct communication with Infinite Intelligence. It is the faculty through which "hunches" and "inspirations" are received. It is by this faculty that all basic, or new, ideas are handed over to man. It is through this faculty that one individual may "tune in" or communicate with the subconscious minds of other men.

The great leaders of business, industry, finance, and the great artists, musicians, poets, and writers, became great because they developed creative imagination.

On the other hand, what Hill calls creative imagination involves tapping into something beyond the information and ideas you have in your mind. You are using creative imagination when you get a flash of insight or inspiration that comes to you completely out of the blue. At the most rarified level, it is what scientists and inventors tap into when they create new systems or discover laws of nature that previously were unknown. More commonly, it occurs in the same way that was referred to in the preceding chapter on Infinite Intelligence: when you get a hunch, a gut feeling, or a premonition about something that turns out to be right, but you had no way of knowing in advance that it would happen.

CREATIVE VISION

In his later writings, Hill devoted less attention to the difference between synthesized and creative imagination, and he began using a new term: *creative vision.* Creative vision is a blending of the conscious mind's imagination with the subconscious mind's intuition.

What this means in a practical sense is that in addition to trying to come up with an idea by consciously attempting to fit together bits and pieces of information in your imagination, you also intentionally encourage your intuitive subconscious to influence the solution.

ssS$ $ss

Transformation of the intangible impulse, of desire, into the tangible reality, of money, calls for the use of a plan, or plans. These plans must be formed with the aid of the imagination, and mainly with the synthetic faculty.

Put your imagination to work creating plans. Commit your plans to writing. The moment you reduce the statement of your desire and a plan for its realization to writing, you will have definitely given concrete form to the intangible desire, and you have actually taken the first in a series of steps that will enable you to convert the thought into its physical counterpart.

ssS$ $ss

MAN'S ONLY LIMITATION, WITHIN REASON, LIES IN THE DEVELOPMENT AND USE OF HIS IMAGINATION.

Synthetic imagination is what will be used most frequently in the process of transforming the impulse of desire into money.

Desire is thought impulse!

Thought impulses are forms of energy.

When you begin with the thought impulse to accumulate money, you are drafting into your service the same "stuff" that nature used in creating this earth, and every material form in the universe, including the body and brain in which the thought impulses function.

IDEAS CAN BE TRANSMUTED INTO CASH THROUGH THE POWER OF A DEFINITE PURPOSE, PLUS DEFINITE PLANS.

Ideas are the beginning points of all fortunes. Ideas are products of the imagination.

Generally speaking, an idea is an impulse of thought that impels action by an appeal to the imagination. All master salespeople know that ideas can be sold where merchandise cannot. Ordinary salespeople do not know this—that is why they are "ordinary."

ss$$$$zzz

The story of practically every great fortune starts with the day when a creator of ideas and a seller of ideas got together and worked in harmony.

Andrew Carnegie surrounded himself with men who could do all that he could *not* do—men who created ideas, and men who put ideas into operation—and he made himself and the others fabulously rich.

ss$$$$zzz

A publisher of books made a discovery that should be worth much to publishers generally. He learned that many people buy titles, and not contents of books.

By merely changing the name of one book that was not moving, his sales on that book jumped upward more than a million copies.

The inside of the book was not changed in any way. He merely ripped off the cover bearing the title that did not sell, and put on a new cover with a title that had "box-office" value.

That, as simple as it may seem, was an IDEA! It was IMAGINATION. There is no standard price on ideas. The creator of ideas makes their own price and, if they are smart, gets it.

ss$$$$zzz

YOU WILL HAVE TO PUSH
TO GET YOUR IDEA STARTED,
BUT THEN YOUR IDEA TAKES OVER
AND PUSHES YOU

When the idea to write the philosophy of personal achievement was first planted in my mind by Mr. Carnegie, it was coaxed, nursed, and enticed to remain alive. Gradually, the idea became a giant under its own power, and it coaxed, nursed, and drove me.

Ideas are like that. First you give life and action and guidance to ideas, then they take on power of their own and sweep aside all opposition.

sss$ $$ss

Chapter 9

ORGANIZED PLANNING:
The Crystallization of Desire into Action

The Sixth Step Toward Riches

We see people who have accumulated great fortunes, but we often recognize only their triumph, overlooking the temporary defeats they had to surmount before "arriving."

No follower of this philosophy can reasonably expect to accumulate a fortune without experiencing "temporary defeat." When defeat comes, accept it as a signal that your plans are not sound, rebuild those plans, and set sail once more toward your coveted goal. If you give up before your goal has been reached, you are a "quitter." Your achievement can be no greater than your plans are sound.

No one is ever whipped until they quit in their own mind.

YOU WILL NEVER ACHIEVE
BIG SUCCESS BY YOURSELF

No individual has sufficient experience, education, native ability, and knowledge to ensure the accumulation of a great fortune without the cooperation of other people. Every plan you adopt in your endeavor to accumulate wealth should be the joint creation of yourself and every other member of your Master Mind group. You may originate your own plans, either in whole or in part, but see that those plans are checked and approved by the members of your Master Mind alliance.

1. Ally yourself with a group of as many people as you may need for the creation and carrying out of your plan or plans for the accumulation of money.

2. Before forming your Master Mind alliance, decide what advantages, and what benefits, you may offer the individual members of your group in return for their cooperation. No one will work indefinitely without some form of compensation.

3. Arrange to meet with the members of your Master Mind group at least twice a week, and more often if possible.

4. Maintain perfect harmony between yourself and every member of your Master Mind group. If you fail to carry out this instruction to the letter, you may expect to meet with failure.

A QUITTER NEVER WINS—
AND A WINNER NEVER QUITS

If the first plan you adopt does not work successfully, replace it with a new plan. If this new plan fails to work, replace it in turn with still another, and so on, until you find a plan which does work.

Right here is the point at which the majority of people meet with failure, because of their lack of persistence in creating new plans to take the place of those that fail.

The most intelligent person living cannot succeed in accumulating money—nor in any other undertaking—without plans that are practical and workable. Just keep this fact in mind, and remember, when your plans fail, that temporary defeat is not permanent failure. It may only mean that your plans have not been sound. Build other plans. Start all over again.

Thomas A. Edison "failed" ten thousand times before he perfected the electric light bulb. That is, he met with temporary defeat ten thousand times—before his success.

Temporary defeat should mean only one thing: the certain knowledge that there is something wrong with your plan. Millions of people go through life in misery and poverty because they lack a sound plan through which to accumulate a fortune.

The successful leader knows that they must plan their work, and work their plan.

LEADERS AND FOLLOWERS

Broadly speaking, there are two types of people in the world. One type is known as leaders and the other as followers.

It is no disgrace to be a follower. On the other hand, it is no credit to *remain* a follower.

With few exceptions, the person who cannot follow a leader intelligently cannot become an efficient leader. An intelligent follower has many advantages, among them the opportunity to acquire knowledge from their leader.

THE MAJOR ATTRIBUTES OF LEADERSHIP

1. UNWAVERING COURAGE. No follower wishes to be dominated by a leader who lacks self-confidence and courage.

2. SELF-CONTROL. Self-control sets a mighty example for one's followers, which the more intelligent will emulate.

3. KEEN SENSE OF JUSTICE. Without a sense of fairness and justice, no leader can command and retain the respect of their followers.

4. DEFINITENESS OF DECISION. The person who wavers in their decisions shows that they are not sure of themself.

5. DEFINITENESS OF PLANS. A leader who moves by guessing is a ship without a rudder, and will land on the rocks.

6. THE HABIT OF DOING MORE THAN PAID FOR. One of the penalties of leadership is to do more than is required of their followers.

7. PLEASING PERSONALITY. No slovenly, careless person can become a successful leader. Leadership calls for respect.

8. SYMPATHY AND UNDERSTANDING. The successful leader must be in sympathy with their followers. Moreover, they must understand them and their problems.

9. MASTERY OF DETAIL. Successful leadership calls for the mastery of details of the leader's position.

10. THE WILLINGNESS TO ASSUME RESPONSIBILITY. If one of the followers makes a mistake and shows themself incompetent, the leader must consider that it is they who failed.

11. COOPERATION. Leadership calls for power, and power calls for cooperation.

THE MAJOR CAUSES OF FAILURE IN LEADERSHIP

It is just as important to know what *not* to do as it is to know what *to* do.

I. INABILITY TO ORGANIZE DETAILS. No real leader is ever "too busy." The successful leader must be the master of all details, including delegating details to capable lieutenants.

2. UNWILLINGNESS TO RENDER HUMBLE SERVICE. Truly great leaders are willing to perform any sort of labor that they would ask another to perform.

3. EXPECTATION OF PAY FOR WHAT THEY "KNOW." The world does not pay people for what they "know." It pays them for what they DO or induce others to do.

4. FEAR OF COMPETITION FROM FOLLOWERS. The able leader trains understudies to whom they may delegate at will. In this way, a leader multiplies himself or herself, and gives attention to many things at one time.

5. LACK OF IMAGINATION. Without imagination, a leader is incapable of meeting emergencies and of creating plans by which to guide their followers.

6. SELFISHNESS. The great leader claims none of the honors. They are content to see the honors go to their followers, because they know that most will work harder for commendation and recognition than they will for money alone.

7. INTEMPERANCE. Followers do not respect an intemperate leader. Moreover, intemperance in any of its forms destroys the endurance and vitality of all who indulge in it.

8. DISLOYALTY. The leader who is not loyal to those above them, *and* those below, cannot long maintain their leadership. Lack of loyalty is one of the major causes of failure in every walk of life

9. EMPHASIS OF THE "AUTHORITY" OF LEADERSHIP. The efficient leader leads by encouraging, and not by trying to instill fear in the hearts of their followers. If a leader is a real leader, they will have no need to advertise that fact except by their conduct—their sympathy, understanding, and fairness.

10. EMPHASIS OF TITLE. The doors to the office of the real leader are open to all who wish to enter, and their working quarters are free from formality or ostentation.

PLANNING TO MARKET YOUR PERSONAL SERVICES

In this chapter Hill presents a self-analysis questionnaire and advice on applying for a job, which are too lengthy to present in an overview, but he also offers the following short comments that neatly capture the importance of organized planning in marketing personal services:

Practically all the great fortunes began in the form of compensation for personal services, or from the sale of ideas.

ss$$ $$zz

The person whose income is derived entirely from the sale of personal services is no less a merchant than the one who sells commodities, and it might well be added that such a person is subject to exactly the same rules of conduct as the merchant who sells merchandise.

ss$$ $$zz

The oldest of admonitions is "Man, know thyself!" If you market merchandise successfully, you must know the merchandise. The same is true in marketing personal services.

You should know all of your weaknesses in order that you may either bridge them or eliminate them entirely.

You should know your strengths in order that you may call attention to them when selling your services. You can know yourself only through accurate analysis.

It is one thing to WANT money—everyone wants more—but it is something entirely different to be WORTH MORE! Many people mistake their wants for their just dues.

ss$$¢¢¢¢

Your financial requirements or wants have nothing whatever to do with your worth. Your value is established entirely by your ability to render useful service or your capacity to induce others to render such service.

ss$$¢¢¢¢

It is an eternal truth that men receive more pay for their ability to get others to perform than they could possibly earn by their own efforts.

ss$$¢¢¢¢

Competent "brains," if effectively marketed, represent a much more desirable form of capital than what is required to conduct a business dealing in commodities, because brains are a form of capital that cannot be depreciated through depressions, nor can they be stolen or spent.

ss$$¢¢¢¢

The day of the "go-getter" has passed. He has been supplanted by the "go-giver." You cannot sow thistles and expect to reap a harvest of grain. You cannot get without giving.

WHERE AND HOW TO FIND OPPORTUNITIES TO ACCUMULATE RICHES

Now that we have analyzed the principles by which riches may be accumulated, we naturally ask, "Where may one find favorable opportunities to apply these principles?" Very well, let us take inventory and see what the United States of America offers the person seeking riches great or small.

Beginning with those words, Napoleon Hill closes this chapter with a ringing testament to the freedoms, privileges, advantages, and opportunities each of us enjoys, and which he attributes to . . .

. . . a mysterious, abstract, greatly misunderstood "something" which gives to every citizen of America more blessings, more opportunities to accumulate wealth, more freedom of every nature, than may be found in any other country.

The name of this mysterious benefactor of mankind is capital!

Capital consists not alone of money but more particularly of highly organized, intelligent groups of scientists, educators, chemists, inventors, business analysts, publicity men, transportation experts, accountants, lawyers, and doctors who have highly specialized knowledge and who pioneer, experiment, and blaze trails in new fields of endeavor.

As an illustration of the importance of capital, Hill describes a typical New York family sitting down to have breakfast:

Some slight idea of the importance of organized capital may be had by trying to imagine yourself burdened with the responsibility of collecting, without the aid of capital, and delivering to the New York City family, a simple breakfast.

Hill then goes on to describe the difficulties of getting eggs from one farmer and bacon from another, going to Florida for oranges, then to Kansas for wheat to make bread, swimming to China for tea, then to Brazil for coffee, somewhere else for bananas, another place for sugar, and so on and so on.

Seems absurd, doesn't it? Well, the procedure described would be the only possible way these simple items of food could be delivered to the heart of New York City if we had no capitalistic system.

The sum of money required for the building and maintenance of the railroads and steamships used in the delivery of that simple breakfast is so huge that it staggers one's imagination. It runs into hundreds of millions of dollars.

Steamships and railroads do not spring up from the earth and function automatically. They come in response to the call of civilization, through the labor and ingenuity and organizing ability of those who have imagination, faith, enthusiasm, decision, persistence! They are known as capitalists. They are motivated by the desire to build, construct, achieve, render useful service, earn profits, and accumulate riches. And because they render service without which there would be no civilization, they put themselves in the way of great riches.

The purpose of this book—a purpose to which I have faithfully devoted over a quarter of a century—is to present to all who want the knowledge, the most dependable philosophy through which individuals may accumulate riches in whatever amounts they desire.

Opportunity has spread its wares before you. Step up to the front, select what you want, create your plan, put the plan into action, and follow through with persistence.

"Capitalistic" America will do the rest.

You can depend on this much: capitalistic America ensures every person the opportunity to render useful service and to collect riches in proportion to the value of the service.

Chapter 10

DECISION:
The Mastery of Procrastination

The Seventh Step Toward Riches

Accurate analysis of over 25,000 men and women who had experienced failure disclosed the fact that lack of decision was near the head of the list of the thirty major causes of failure.

Procrastination—the opposite of decision—is a common enemy that practically everyone must conquer.

Analysis of several hundred people who had accumulated fortunes well beyond the million-dollar mark disclosed the fact that every one of them had the habit of reaching decisions promptly and of changing these decisions slowly.

The people who fail to accumulate money have the habit of reaching decisions very slowly and of changing these decisions quickly and often.

The majority of people who fail to accumulate money sufficient for their needs are, generally, easily influenced by the "opinions" of others. They permit the newspapers and the "gossiping" neighbors to do their "thinking" for them.

Opinions are the cheapest commodities on earth. Everyone has a flock of opinions ready to be wished upon anyone who will accept them.

ss$$ $$ss

Close friends and relatives, while not meaning to do so, often handicap one through "opinions" and sometimes through ridicule, which is meant to be humorous.

Thousands of men and women carry inferiority complexes with them all through life, because some well-meaning but ignorant person destroyed their confidence through "opinions" or ridicule.

ss$$ $$ss

If you need facts or information from other people to enable you to reach decisions, acquire these facts or secure the information you need quietly, without disclosing your purpose.

ss$$ $$ss

Keep your eyes and ears wide open, and your mouth closed, if you wish to acquire the habit of prompt decision. Those who talk too much do little else.

If you talk more than you listen, you not only deprive yourself of many opportunities to accumulate useful knowledge, but you also disclose your plans and purposes to people who will take great delight in defeating you, because they envy you.

ssSSss

Remember, also, that every time you open your mouth in the presence of a person who has an abundance of knowledge, you display to that person your exact stock of knowledge, or your lack of it! Genuine wisdom is usually conspicuous through modesty and silence.

ssSSss

Let one of your first decisions be to keep a closed mouth and open ears and eyes.

As a reminder to yourself to follow this advice, it will be helpful if you copy the following epigram in large letters and place it where you will see it daily:

> ## TELL THE WORLD WHAT YOU INTEND TO DO, BUT FIRST SHOW IT.
>
> ## DEEDS AND NOT WORDS ARE WHAT COUNT MOST

FREEDOM OR DEATH ON A DECISION

To emphasize his point about the need for firm decision, Napoleon Hill tells his interpretation of the events leading to the signing of the Declaration of Independence. In Hill's view, the fifty-six men who signed were the world's greatest Master Mind alliance.

Analyze the events that led to the Declaration of Independence, and be convinced that this nation, which now holds a position of commanding respect and power among all nations of the world, was born of a DECISION created by a Master Mind consisting of fifty-six men. Note well that it was their DECISION which ensured the success of Washington's armies, because the spirit of that decision was in the heart of every soldier who fought with him and served as a spiritual power that recognizes no such thing as FAILURE.

Note that the power which gave this nation its freedom is the self-same power that must be used by every individual who becomes self-determining.

Throughout this philosophy will be found the suggestion that thought—backed by strong desire—has a tendency to transmute itself into its physical equivalent. You may find in this story a perfect description of the method by which thought makes this astounding transformation.

In your search for the secret of the method, do not look for a miracle, because you will not find it. You will find only the eternal laws of nature. These laws are available to every person who has the faith and the courage to use them. They may be used to bring freedom to a nation, or to accumulate riches.

Keep your own counsel, when you begin to put into practice the principles described here, by reaching your own decisions and following them. Take no one into your confidence, except the members of your Master Mind group, and be very sure in your selection of this group that you choose only those who will be in complete sympathy and harmony with your purpose.

Those who reach decisions promptly and definitely, know what they want and generally get it. The leaders in every walk of life decide quickly and firmly. That is the major reason why they are leaders. The world has a habit of making room for those whose words and actions show that they know where they are going.

Indecision is a habit which usually begins in youth. The major weakness of all educational systems is that they neither teach nor encourage the habit of definite decision.

~ $ ~

The habit of indecision acquired because of the deficiencies of our school systems goes with the student into the occupation he chooses . . . IF, in fact, he chooses his occupation. Generally, the youth just out of school seeks any job that can be found. He takes the first place he finds, because he has fallen into the habit of indecision.

~ $ ~

Definiteness of decision always requires courage, sometimes very great courage. The fifty-six men who signed the Declaration of Independence staked their lives on the decision to affix their signatures to that document.

~ $ ~

The person who reaches a definite decision to procure a particular job and make life pay the price asked, does not stake their life on that decision; they stake their economic freedom. The person who desires riches in the same spirit that Samuel Adams desired freedom for the Colonies, is sure to accumulate wealth.

~ $ ~

Chapter 11

PERSISTENCE:
The Sustained Effort
Necessary to Induce Faith

The Eighth Step Toward Riches

Persistence is an essential factor in the procedure of transmuting desire into its monetary equivalent. The basis of persistence is the power of will.

Willpower and desire, when properly combined, make an irresistible pair.

There may be no heroic connotation to the word *persistence*, but this quality is to the character of a person what carbon is to steel.

The starting point of all achievement is desire. Weak desires bring weak results, just as a small amount of fire makes a small amount of heat. If you are lacking in persistence, this weakness may be remedied by building a stronger fire under your desires.

One thing we all know, if one does not possess persistence, one does not achieve noteworthy success in any calling.

$ss\$\$ \$\$ss$

There is no substitute for persistence! It cannot be supplanted by any other quality! Remember this, and it will hearten you in the beginning when the going may seem difficult and slow.

$ss\$\$ \$\$ss$

Those who pick themselves up after defeat, and keep on trying, arrive; and the world cries, "Bravo! I knew you could do it!"

Those who can "take it" are bountifully rewarded for their persistence. They receive something infinitely more important than material compensation: the knowledge that "every failure brings with it the seed of an equivalent advantage."

$ss\$\$ \$\$ss$

Persistence is a state of mind. Therefore, it can be cultivated. Like all states of mind, persistence is the direct result of habit. The mind absorbs the daily experiences on which it feeds. Fear can be cured by forced repetition of acts of courage.

$ss\$\$ \$\$ss$

Occasional effort to apply the rules will be of no value to you. To get results, you must apply all of the rules until their application becomes a fixed habit with you. In no other way can you develop the necessary "money consciousness."

> # YOU HAVE TO WORK AT CREATING MONEY CONSCIOUSNESS.
>
> # POVERTY CONSCIOUSNESS TAKES OVER WITHOUT EVEN TRYING.

ssSS SSss

Poverty is attracted to the one whose mind is favorable to it, as money is attracted to the one whose mind has been deliberately prepared to attract it—and through the same laws.

ssSS SSss

Poverty consciousness will voluntarily seize the mind which is not occupied with money consciousness.

ssSS SSss

Poverty consciousness develops without conscious application. Money consciousness must be created to order.

ssSS SSss

Fortunes gravitate to those whose minds have been prepared to "attract" them, just as surely as water gravitates to the ocean. In this book may be found all the stimuli necessary to "attune" any normal mind to the vibrations that will attract the object of one's desires.

SYMPTOMS OF A LACK OF PERSISTENCE

1. A failure to clearly define exactly what one wants

2. Procrastination

3. Lack of interest in acquiring specialized knowledge

4. Indecision

5. The habit of relying on alibis

6. Self-satisfaction

7. Indifference; readiness to compromise rather than fight

8. The habit of blaming others for one's mistakes

9. Weakness of desire

10. Willingness to quit at the first sign of defeat

11. Lack of organized plans placed in writing

12. Neglecting to move on ideas or grasp opportunity

13. Wishing instead of willing

14. Compromising with poverty instead of aiming at riches

15. Trying to get without giving

16. Fear of criticism

FEAR OF WHAT OTHERS WILL THINK, SAY, OR DO

When Andrew Carnegie suggested that I devote twenty years to the organization of a philosophy of individual achievement, my first impulse of thought was fear of what people might say.

As quick as a flash, my mind began to create alibis and excuses, all of them traceable to the inherent fear of criticism. Something inside of me said, "You can't do it; the job is too big and requires too much time—What will your relatives think of you?—How will you earn a living?—No one has ever organized a philosophy of success; what right have you to believe you can do it?—Who are you anyway, to aim so high?—Remember your humble birth; what do you know about philosophy?—People will think you are crazy (and they did)—Why hasn't some other person done this before now?"

It seemed as if the whole world had suddenly turned its attention to me with the purpose of ridiculing me into giving up all desire to carry out Mr. Carnegie's suggestion.

ss$$S2ss

The majority of people permit relatives, friends, and the public at large to so influence them that they cannot live their own lives because they fear criticism.

Huge numbers of people make mistakes in marriage, and go through life miserable and unhappy, because they fear criticism.

Millions of people neglect to acquire belated educations after having left school, because they fear criticism.

Countless numbers of men and women permit relatives to wreck their lives in the name of duty, because they fear criticism. (Duty does not require any person to submit to the destruction of personal ambitions and the right to live their own life in their own way.)

People refuse to take chances in business, because they fear the criticism that may follow if they fail. The fear of criticism, in such cases, is stronger than the desire for success.

ss$$$ 2̂222

After having analyzed thousands of people, I discovered that most ideas are still-born and need the breath of life injected into them through definite plans of immediate action.

The time to nurse an idea is at the time of its birth. Every minute it lives gives it a better chance of surviving. The fear of criticism is at the bottom of the destruction of most ideas that never reach the planning and action stage.

ss$$$ 2̂222

Ask the first hundred people you meet what they want most in life, and ninety-eight of them will not be able to tell you. If you press them for an answer, some will say security; many will say money; a few will say happiness; others will say fame and power;

and still others will say social recognition; ease of living; ability to sing, dance, or write.

But none of them will be able to define these terms, or give the slightest indication of a plan by which they hope to attain these vaguely expressed wishes.

Riches do not respond to wishes. They respond only to definite plans, backed by definite desires, through constant persistence.

ss$$&&ss

HOW TO DEVELOP PERSISTENCE

There are four steps that lead to the habit of persistence:

1. A definite purpose, backed by a burning desire for its fulfillment.

2. A definite plan, expressed in continuous action.

3. A mind closed tightly against all negative and discouraging influences including negative suggestions of relatives, friends, and acquaintances.

4. A friendly alliance with one or more persons who encourage you to follow through with both plan and purpose.

There is a magnificent reward for all who learn to take these four steps. It is the privilege of writing one's own ticket and of making life yield whatever price is asked.

ss$$&&ss

Chapter 12

POWER OF THE MASTER MIND:
The Driving Force

The Ninth Step Toward Riches

Power is essential for success in the accumulation of money.

Power, as the term is here used, refers to organized effort sufficient to enable an individual to transmute desire into its monetary equivalent. Plans are inert and useless without sufficient power to translate them into action.

This chapter will describe the method by which an individual may attain and apply power. Power may be defined as "organized and intelligently directed knowledge."

Organized effort is produced through the coordination of effort of two or more people, who work toward a definite end, in a spirit of harmony.

GAINING POWER THROUGH THE MASTER MIND

The Master Mind may be defined as "coordination of knowledge and effort, in a spirit of harmony, between two or more people, for the attainment of a definite purpose."

No individual may have great power without availing themself of the Master Mind.

THERE ARE TWO ASPECTS TO THE MASTER MIND; ONE IS ECONOMIC, THE OTHER IS PSYCHIC

I. ECONOMIC: Economic advantages may be created by any person who surrounds themself with the advice and personal cooperation of a group of people who are willing to lend them wholehearted aid, in a spirit of perfect harmony. This form of cooperative alliance has been the basis of every great fortune.

The Master Mind principle, or rather the economic feature of it, was first called to my attention by Andrew Carnegie, over twenty-five years ago. Discovery of this principle was responsible for the choice of my life's work.

Mr. Carnegie's Master Mind group consisted of a staff of approximately fifty men, with whom he surrounded himself for the definite purpose of manufacturing and marketing steel. He attributed his entire fortune to the power he accumulated through this Master Mind.

Analyze the record of anyone who has accumulated a great fortune, and you will find that they have either consciously, or unconsciously, employed the Master Mind principle.

2. PSYCHIC: The psychic phase of the Master Mind principle is much more abstract. You may catch a significant suggestion from this statement: No two minds ever come together without thereby creating a third invisible, intangible force which may be likened to a third mind.

Energy is nature's universal set of building blocks, out of which she constructs every material thing in the universe, including man. Nature's building blocks are available to man in the energy involved in thinking!

Man's brain may be compared to an electric battery. It is a well-known fact that a group of electric batteries will provide more energy than a single battery.

It is also a well-known fact that an individual battery will provide energy in proportion to the number and capacity of the cells it contains.

The brain functions in a similar fashion. A group of brains, coordinated (or connected) in a spirit of harmony, will provide more thought-energy than a single brain, just as a group of electric batteries will provide more energy than a single battery.

When a group of individual brains are coordinated and function in harmony, the increased energy created through that alliance becomes available to every individual brain in the group.

The human mind is a form of energy, a part of it being spiritual in nature. When the minds of two people are coordinated in a spirit of harmony, the spiritual units of energy of each mind form an affinity which constitutes the "psychic" phase of the Master Mind.

When two or more people coordinate in a spirit of harmony and work toward a definite objective, they place themselves in position, through that alliance, to absorb power directly from the great universal storehouse of Infinite Intelligence.

This is the greatest of all sources of power. It is the source to which the genius turns. It is the source to which every great leader turns (whether they may be conscious of the fact or not).

⸎ $ ⸎

HENRY FORD RELIED UPON
HIS MASTER MIND GROUP

Henry Ford began his business career under the handicap of poverty, illiteracy, and ignorance. It is a fact that within the inconceivably short period of ten years Mr. Ford mastered these three handicaps, and that within twenty-five years he made himself one of the richest men in America.

Henry Ford whipped poverty, illiteracy, and ignorance by allying himself with great minds, whose vibrations of thought he absorbed into his own mind.

Through his association with Edison, Burbank, Burroughs, and Firestone, Mr. Ford added to his own brain power the sum and substance of the intelligence, experience, knowledge, and spiritual forces of these four men.

Moreover, he appropriated and made use of the Master Mind principle through the methods of procedure described in this book.

> Men take on the nature and the habits and the power of thought of those with whom they associate in a spirit of sympathy and harmony.

CREATING YOUR OWN MASTER MIND

As a reminder, the following explanation of the basis of the Master Mind is reprinted from chapter 9, Organized Planning.

I. Ally yourself with a group of as many people as you may need for the creation and carrying out of your plan or plans for the accumulation of money—making use of the Master Mind principle.

2. Before forming your Master Mind alliance, decide what advantages, and what benefits, you may offer the individual members of your group in return for their cooperation. No intelligent person will either request or expect another to work without adequate compensation, although this may not always be in the form of money.

3. Arrange to meet with the members of your Master Mind group at least twice a week, and more often if possible, until you have jointly perfected the necessary plan.

4. You must maintain perfect harmony between yourself and every member of your Master Mind group. The Master Mind principle cannot work without perfect harmony.

No individual has sufficient experience, education, native ability, and knowledge to ensure the accumulation of a great fortune without the cooperation of other people. Every plan you adopt in your endeavor to accumulate wealth should be the joint creation of yourself and every other member of your Master Mind group. You may originate your own plans, either in whole or in part, but see that those plans are checked and approved by the members of your Master Mind alliance.

$$ss\$\$ \,\, \$\$ss$$

Chapter 13

THE MYSTERY OF SEX TRANSMUTATION

The Tenth Step Toward Riches

The meaning of the word *transmute* is, in simple language, "the changing or transferring of one element, or form of energy, into another."

Sex transmutation is simple and easily explained. It means the switching of the mind from thoughts of physical expression to thoughts of some other nature.

Sexual desire is the most powerful of human desires. When driven by this desire, men develop keenness of imagination, courage, willpower, persistence, and creative ability unknown to them at other times. So strong and impelling is the desire for sexual contact that men freely run the risk of life and reputation to indulge it.

THE 10 MIND STIMULI

The human mind responds to stimuli through which it may be "keyed up" to high rates of enthusiasm, creative imagination, intense desire, etc. The stimuli to which the mind responds most freely are the following:

1. The desire for sexual expression

2. Love

3. A burning desire for fame, power, or financial gain

4. Music

5. Friendship between either those of the same sex or those of the opposite sex

6. A Master Mind alliance based on the harmony of two or more people who ally themselves for advancement

7. Mutual suffering, such as that experienced by people who are persecuted

8. Autosuggestion

9. Fear

10. Narcotics and alcohol

The desire for sexual expression comes at the head of the list of stimuli which most effectively "step up" the vibrations of the mind and start the "wheels" of physical action.

This desire cannot and should not be submerged or eliminated, but it should be given an outlet through forms of expression that enrich the body, mind, and spirit of man. If not given this form of outlet through transmutation, it will seek outlets through purely physical channels.

ss$$ $$zz

The emotion of sex contains the secret of creative ability. Destroy the sex glands, whether in man or in beast, and you have removed the major source of action. For proof of this, observe what happens to any animal after it has been castrated.

ss$$ $$zz

When harnessed and redirected along other lines, sexual emotion may be used as a powerful creative force in literature, art, or in any other profession or calling including, of course, the accumulation of riches.

ss$$ $$zz

The pages of history are filled with the records of great leaders whose achievements may be traced directly to the influence of women who aroused the creative faculties of their minds, through the stimulation of sexual desire.

CREATIVE IMAGINATION IS THE SIXTH SENSE

When brain action has been stimulated it has the effect of lifting the individual far above the horizon of ordinary thought. While on this exalted plane, the creative faculty of the mind is given freedom for action. The way has been cleared for the "sixth sense" to function and it becomes receptive to ideas that could not reach the individual under any other circumstances.

ss$$ $$ss

This sixth sense is *creative imagination.* The faculty of creative imagination is the direct link between the finite mind of man and Infinite Intelligence. All revelations, and all discoveries of basic or new principles in the field of invention, take place through the faculty of creative imagination.

ss$$ $$ss

The great artists, writers, musicians, and poets become great because they acquire the habit of relying upon the "still small voice" that speaks from within through the faculty of creative imagination. It is a fact well known to people who have keen imaginations, that their best ideas come through so-called "hunches."

ss$$ $$ss

The sixth sense is the faculty that marks the difference between a genius and an ordinary individual.

SEXUAL ENERGY = CHARISMA

The world is ruled, and the destiny of civilization is established, by the human emotions. People are influenced in their actions not by reason so much as by "feelings." The creative faculty of the mind is set into action entirely by emotions and not by cold reason. The most powerful of human emotions is that of sex.

ss$\$$ 2ss

A teacher who has trained and directed the efforts of more than 30,000 salespeople made the astounding discovery that highly sexed men are the most efficient salesmen. The explanation is that the factor of personality known as "personal magnetism" is nothing more nor less than sexual energy.

When employing salesmen, the more capable sales manager looks for the quality of personal magnetism as the first requirement. People who lack sexual energy will never become enthusiastic nor inspire others with enthusiasm, and enthusiasm is one of the most important requisites in salesmanship.

The public speaker, orator, preacher, lawyer, or salesman who is lacking sexual energy or charisma is a "flop," as far as being able to influence others is concerned. Couple with this the fact that most people can be influenced only through an appeal to their emotions, and you will understand the importance of sexual energy as a part of the salesman's native ability.

Through cultivation and understanding, sexual energy or charisma may be drawn upon and used to great advantage in your interaction with others. This energy may be communicated in the following ways:

1. The handshake. The touch of the hand indicates, instantly, the presence of magnetism, or the lack of it.

2. The tone of voice. Magnetism, or sex energy, is the factor with which the voice may be colored, or made musical and charming.

3. Posture and carriage of the body. Highly sexed people move briskly, and with grace and ease.

4. The vibrations of thought. Highly sexed people mix the emotion of sex with their thoughts, or may do so at will, and in that way may influence those around them.

5. Personal appearance. They usually select clothing of a style becoming to their personality, physique, complexion, etc.

ssS$ꝃꝃꝃ

Master salesmen attain the status of mastery because they transmute the energy of sex into sales enthusiasm. The majority of salesmen do so without being in the least aware of what they are doing, or how they are doing it.

ssS$ꝃꝃꝃ

SEX IS BIOLOGY, LOVE IS PSYCHOLOGY

When driven by his desire to please a woman, based solely on the emotion of sex, a man may be capable of great achievement —but his actions may be disorganized, distorted, and totally destructive. He may steal, cheat, and even commit murder.

But when the emotion of love is mixed with the emotion of sex, that same man will guide his actions with more sanity, balance, and reason.

The road to genius consists of the development, control, and use of sex, love, and romance.

- Encourage the presence of these emotions as the dominating thoughts in one's mind, and discourage the presence of all the destructive emotions. The mind is a creature of habit. It thrives on the dominating thoughts fed to it.

- Control comes from persistence and habit. The secret of control lies in understanding the process of transmutation. When any negative emotion presents itself in one's mind, it can be transmuted into a positive or constructive emotion, by the simple procedure of changing one's thoughts.

Love, romance, and sex are all emotions capable of driving men to heights of superachievement. Love is the emotion that serves as a safety valve, and ensures balance, poise, and constructive effort.

ssSS SSss

Chapter 14

THE SUBCONSCIOUS MIND:
The Connecting Link.

The Eleventh Step Toward Riches

The subconscious mind consists of a field of consciousness in which every impulse of thought that reaches the objective mind through any of the five senses is classified and recorded, and from which thoughts may be recalled or withdrawn, as letters may be taken from a filing cabinet.

It receives and files sense impressions or thoughts, regardless of their nature. You may voluntarily plant in your subconscious mind any plan, thought, or purpose that you desire to translate into its physical or monetary equivalent. The subconscious acts first on the dominating desires which have been mixed with emotional feeling, such as faith.

THOUGHTS ARE THINGS

Thoughts are truly things, for the reason that every material thing begins in the form of thought-energy.

Everything that man creates begins in the form of a thought impulse. Through the aid of the imagination, thought impulses may be assembled into plans.

ss$$ẕẕss

You cannot entirely control your subconscious mind, but you can voluntarily hand over to it any plan, desire, or purpose that you wish transformed into concrete form.

ss$$ẕẕss

All thought impulses intended for transmutation into their physical equivalent must pass through the imagination and be mixed with faith. The "mixing" of faith with a plan or purpose, for submission to the subconscious mind, may be done ONLY through the imagination.

ss$$ẕẕss

Through a method of procedure unknown to man, the subconscious mind draws upon the forces of Infinite Intelligence for the power with which it voluntarily transmutes one's desires into their physical equivalent, making use always of the most practical media by which this end may be accomplished.

As was noted in the opening chapter, What You Need to Know, Napoleon Hill's explanation of the way in which Infinite Intelligence can transmute thoughts into reality is this: By planting positive thoughts in your subconscious, you change the way you think; and by changing the way you think, you change the way you act; and by changing the way you act, you can make things happen in reality.

ss$$ $$$$zz

After you have accepted, as a reality, the existence of the subconscious mind and understand its possibilities as a medium for transmuting your desires into their physical or monetary equivalent, you will understand why you have to make your desires clear and reduce them to writing.

ss$$ $$$$zz

Remember that your subconscious mind functions voluntarily, whether you make any effort to influence it or not. If you fail to plant desires in your subconscious mind, it will feed on the thoughts that reach it as the result of your neglect.

You are living daily in the midst of all manner of thought impulses which are reaching your subconscious mind without your knowledge. Some of these impulses are negative, some are positive. You are now engaged in trying to help shut off the flow of negative impulses, and to aid in voluntarily influencing your subconscious mind through positive impulses of desire.

The subconscious mind is more susceptible to influence by impulses of thought mixed with "feeling" or emotion than by those originating solely in the reasoning portion of the mind.

It is a well-known fact that emotion or feelings rule the majority of people. If it is true that the subconscious mind responds more quickly to thought impulses that are well mixed with emotion, it is essential to become familiar with the more important of the emotions.

There are seven major positive emotions and seven major negative emotions.

The negatives voluntarily inject themselves into the thought impulses, which ensure passage into the subconscious mind.

The positives must be injected—through the principle of autosuggestion—into the thought impulses that an individual wishes to pass on to their subconscious mind.

You are preparing yourself to influence and control the "inner audience" of your subconscious mind in order to hand over to it the desire for money, which you wish transmuted into its monetary equivalent. It understands best the language of emotion or feeling.

The major emotions are listed on the following page so that you may draw upon the positives, and avoid the negatives, when giving instructions to your subconscious mind.

THE SEVEN MAJOR POSITIVE EMOTIONS

The emotion of DESIRE

The emotion of FAITH

The emotion of LOVE

The emotion of SEX

The emotion of ENTHUSIASM

The emotion of ROMANCE

The emotion of HOPE

THE SEVEN MAJOR NEGATIVE EMOTIONS

The emotion of FEAR

The emotion of JEALOUSY

The emotion of HATRED

The emotion of REVENGE

The emotion of GREED

The emotion of SUPERSTITION

The emotion of ANGER

YOU MAKE THE CHOICE: POSITIVE OR NEGATIVE

Positive and negative emotions cannot occupy the mind at the same time. One or the other must dominate. It is your responsibility to make sure that positive emotions constitute the dominating influence of your mind.

Here the law of habit will come to your aid. Form the habit of applying and using the positive emotions! Eventually, they will dominate your mind so completely that the negatives cannot even enter it.

WHY PRAYERS CAN SOMETIMES PRODUCE NEGATIVE ANSWERS

If you are an observing person, you must have noticed that most people resort to prayer only after everything else has failed! Or else they pray by a ritual of meaningless words. And because it is a fact that most people who pray do so only after everything else has failed, they go to prayer with their minds filled with fear and doubt, which are the emotions the subconscious mind acts upon and passes on to Infinite Intelligence. Likewise, that is the emotion which Infinite Intelligence receives, and also acts upon.

If you pray for a thing, but have fear as you pray that you may not receive it, or that your prayer will not be acted upon by Infinite Intelligence, your prayer will have been in vain.

If you have ever had the experience of receiving what you prayed for, go back in your memory and recall your actual state of mind while you were praying, and you will know, for sure, that the theory here described is more than a theory.

The subconscious mind is the intermediary which translates one's prayers into terms that Infinite Intelligence can recognize, presents the message, and brings back the answer in the form of a definite plan or idea for procuring the object of the prayer.

Understand this principle, and you will know why mere words read from a prayer book cannot and will never serve as an agency of communication between the human mind and Infinite Intelligence.

sss$¢¢¢¢

Chapter 15

THE BRAIN:
A Broadcasting and Receiving Station for Thought

The Twelfth Step Toward Riches

More than twenty years ago, working in conjunction with the late Dr. Alexander Graham Bell and Dr. Elmer R. Gates, I observed that every human brain is both a broadcasting and a receiving station for the vibration of thought.

In a fashion similar to the radio broadcasting principle, every human brain is capable of picking up vibrations of thought that are being released by other brains.

The creative imagination is the "receiving set" of the brain, which receives thoughts released by the brains of others. It is the means of communication between your conscious, or reasoning, mind and the four sources from which you receive the thought stimuli of taste, touch, sight, and smell.

When stimulated or "stepped up" to a high rate of vibration, the mind becomes more receptive to the vibration of thought which reaches it from outside sources. This "stepping up" process takes place through the positive emotions or the negative emotions. Through the emotions, the vibrations of thought may be increased.

ss$$ $$ss

When the brain is vibrating at a rapid rate, it not only attracts thoughts and ideas released by other brains, but it gives to one's own thoughts the "feeling" that is essential before those thoughts will be picked up and acted upon by one's subconscious mind.

ss$$ $$ss

- The subconscious mind is the sending station of the brain through which vibrations of thought are broadcast.

- The creative imagination is the "receiving set" through which the vibrations of thought are picked up from the ether.

- Autosuggestion is the medium by which you may put into operation your "broadcasting" station.

- The stimuli through which you put these three principles into action begins with DESIRE.

THE GREATEST FORCES ARE "INTANGIBLE"

Through the ages which have passed, man has depended too much on his physical senses and has limited his knowledge to physical things that he could see, touch, weigh, and measure.

Sometimes men speak lightly of the intangibles—the things they cannot perceive through any of their five senses—and when we hear them, it should remind us that all of us are controlled by forces that are unseen and intangible.

Mankind has not the power to cope with nor to control the intangible force wrapped up in the rolling waves of the oceans.

Man has not the capacity to understand the intangible force of gravity, which keeps this earth suspended and keeps man from falling from it, much less the power to control that force.

Man is entirely subservient to the intangible force which comes with a thunderstorm, and he is just as helpless in the presence of the intangible force of electricity.

Nor is this the end of man's ignorance in connection with things unseen and intangible. He does not understand the intangible force wrapped up in the soil of the earth—the force that provides him with every morsel of food he eats, every article of clothing he wears, every dollar he carries in his pockets.

Last, but not least, man understands little of the intangible force—the greatest of all the intangibles—of thought.

IT MUST BE MORE THAN JUST WIRING

In this chapter, Hill makes it clear that what medical science has learned about the physical complexity of the human brain has convinced him that the true capability of the human mind is also one of the intangibles that mankind has underestimated.

To support his opinion, Hill cites some of the studies being conducted at that time into extrasensory perception and other psychic phenomena. He then explains his own experiments with the concept of the brain/mind sending and receiving thoughts.

A SIMPLE EXAMPLE, BUT IT WORKS

My associates and I have discovered what we believe to be the ideal conditions under which the mind can be stimulated so that the sixth sense, described in the next chapter, can be made to function in a practical way.

The procedure is very simple. We sit down at a conference table, clearly state the nature of the problem we have under consideration, then begin discussing it. You of course recognize the roundtable procedure here described as being a practical application of the Master Mind.

Through experimentation and practice, we have discovered how to stimulate our minds so that we can, by a process of blending our three minds into one, find the solution to a great variety of personal problems that are submitted by my clients.

The strange thing about this method of mind stimulation is that it places each participant in communication with unknown sources of knowledge definitely outside his own experience.

By adopting and following a similar plan, any student of this philosophy may come into possession of the famous Carnegie formula briefly described in the introduction.

THE BRAIN AND THE MASTER MIND

As was mentioned in the opening chapter, Napoleon Hill theorized that humans sometimes pick up external thought waves that appear in the imagination in the form of hunches or intuitions. The members of a group who are chosen specifically because they share the same definite chief aim are even more likely to make such connections.

- Infinite Intelligence interconnects all things in such a way that whatever you focus on in your mind acts like a magnet, attracting other like-natured ideas.

- A Master Mind is formed when two or more people come together to focus on the same thing, and it is the combination of minds that attracts the creative ideas.

- By definition, the members of a Master Mind are committed to the same philosophy, and with multiple minds focused on the same definite chief aim, all members also have access to a wider, deeper, communal pool of Infinite Intelligence.

The theory of the Master Mind is that two heads are not only better than one, they are better than two—because the combination is greater than the sum of its parts.

No two minds ever come together without creating this third invisible, intangible force which, in the case of a Master Mind, will produce insights and ideas that neither of the individual minds would have come up with independently.

ss$$$$ss

Chapter 16

THE SIXTH SENSE:
The Door to the Temple of Wisdom

The Thirteenth Step Toward Riches

The thirteenth principle is known as the sixth sense, through which Infinite Intelligence may and will communicate voluntarily, without any effort from, or demands by, the individual.

The sixth sense is that portion of the subconscious mind which has been referred to as the creative imagination. It has also been referred to as the "receiving set" through which ideas, plans, and thoughts flash into the mind. Those "flashes" are sometimes called hunches or inspirations.

The sixth sense is the medium of contact between the finite mind of man and Infinite Intelligence, and for this reason it is a mixture of both the mental and the spiritual. It is the point at which the mind of man contacts the Universal Mind.

I DO NOT BELIEVE IN MIRACLES . . .

I am not a believer in nor an advocate of "miracles," for the reason that I have enough knowledge of nature to understand that nature never deviates from her established laws. Some of her laws are so incomprehensible that they produce what appear to be "miracles." The sixth sense comes as near to being a miracle as anything I have ever experienced, and it appears so only because I do not understand the method by which this principle is operated.

. . . HOWEVER, THE HUMAN MIND CAN DO SOME SURPRISING THINGS

This much I do know: that there is a power, or a First Cause, an Intelligence, which permeates every atom of matter, and embraces every unit of energy perceptible to man.

Infinite Intelligence converts acorns into oak trees, causes water to flow downhill in response to the law of gravity, follows night with day and winter with summer, each maintaining its proper place and relationship to the other.

This Intelligence may, through the principles of this philosophy, be induced to aid in transmuting desires into concrete or material form. I have this knowledge because I have experimented with it—and have experienced it.

CHANGE WHAT YOU BELIEVE ABOUT YOURSELF AND YOU CAN CHANGE YOUR REALITY

Long before I had ever written a line for publication, or had endeavored to deliver a speech in public, I followed the habit of reshaping my own character by trying to imitate the nine men whose lives and lifeworks had been most impressive to me. These nine men were Emerson, Paine, Edison, Darwin, Lincoln, Burbank, Napoleon, Ford, and Carnegie.

Every night, over a long period of years, I held an imaginary council meeting with this group whom I called my "Invisible Counselors."

The procedure was this: Just before going to sleep at night I would shut my eyes and see, in my imagination, this group of men seated with me around my council table. Here I had not only an opportunity to sit among those whom I considered to be great, but I actually dominated the group, by serving as the chairman.

My purpose was to rebuild my own character so it would represent a composite of the characters of my imaginary counselors. Realizing, as I did early in life, that I had to overcome the handicap of birth in an environment of ignorance and superstition, I deliberately assigned myself the task of voluntary rebirth through the method here described.

BUILDING CHARACTER
THROUGH AUTOSUGGESTION

Being an earnest student of psychology, I knew that all people become what they are because of their dominating thoughts and desires, and I knew that self-suggestion is a powerful factor in building character.

With this knowledge of the principles of mind operation, I was fairly well armed with the equipment needed in rebuilding my character. In these imaginary council meetings, I called on my cabinet members for the knowledge I wished each to contribute.

After some months of this nightly procedure, I was astounded by the discovery that these imaginary figures developed individual characteristics, which surprised me.

Lest I be misunderstood, I wish here to state most emphatically, that I still regard my cabinet meetings as being purely imaginary, but while the members of my cabinet may be purely fictional, and the meetings existent only in my own imagination, they have led me into glorious paths of adventure, rekindled an appreciation of true greatness, encouraged creative endeavor, and emboldened the expression of honest thought.

My original purpose in conducting council meetings with imaginary beings was solely that of impressing my own subconscious mind, through the principle of autosuggestion, with certain characteristics that I desired to acquire. In more recent years, my experimentation has taken on an entirely different trend. I now go to my imaginary counselors with every difficult problem that confronts me and my clients. The results are often astonishing, although I do not depend entirely on this form of counsel.

GAIN ACCESS TO THOUGHTS AND IDEAS HIDDEN IN YOUR SUBCONSCIOUS

Somewhere in the cell-structure of the brain is located an organ that receives vibrations of thought ordinarily called "hunches." So far, science has not discovered where this organ of the sixth sense is located, but this is not important. The fact remains that human beings do receive accurate knowledge through sources other than the physical senses.

sss$$sss

The sixth sense is not something that one can take off and put on at will. Ability to use this great power comes slowly, through application of the other principles outlined in this book.

sss$$sss

Chapter 17

THE SIX GHOSTS
OF FEAR

Take inventory of yourself as you
read this closing chapter and find out
how many of the "ghosts" are
standing in your way...

Previous chapters have described how to develop faith, through autosuggestion, desire, and the subconscious. This chapter presents detailed instructions for the mastery of fear.

Here will be found a description of the six fears which are the cause of all discouragement, timidity, procrastination, indifference, indecision, and the lack of ambition, self-reliance, initiative, self-control, and enthusiasm.

Search yourself carefully as you study these six enemies, as they may exist only in your subconscious mind, where their presence will be hard to detect.

Remember, as you analyze the Six Ghosts of Fear, that they are nothing but ghosts—*because* they exist only in your mind.

THE SIX BASIC FEARS

There are six basic fears, with some combination of which every human suffers at one time or another. Most people are fortunate if they do not suffer from the entire six. Named in the order of their most common appearance, they are:

1. The fear of POVERTY

2. The fear of CRITICISM

3. The fear of ILL HEALTH

4. The fear of LOSS OF LOVE OF SOMEONE

5. The fear of OLD AGE

6. The fear of DEATH

Fears are nothing more than states of mind. Your state of mind is subject to control and direction.

Nature has endowed man with absolute control over but one thing—and that is thought.

This fact, coupled with the additional fact that everything man creates begins in the form of a thought, leads one very near to the principle by which fear may be mastered.

OLD MAN WORRY

Worry is a form of sustained fear caused by indecision. Therefore it is a state of mind which can be controlled.

An unsettled mind is helpless. Indecision makes an unsettled mind. The six basic fears become translated into a state of worry through indecision.

1. Relieve yourself forever of the fear of death by reaching a decision to accept death as an inescapable event.

2. Whip the fear of poverty by reaching a decision to get along with whatever wealth you can accumulate without worry.

3. Put your foot upon the neck of the fear of criticism by reaching a decision not to worry about what other people think, do, or say.

4. Eliminate the fear of old age by reaching a decision to accept it not as a handicap but as a great blessing which carries with it wisdom, self-control, and understanding not known to youth.

5. Acquit yourself of the fear of ill health by the decision to forget symptoms.

6. Master the fear of loss of love by reaching a decision to get along without love, if that is necessary.

Kill the habit of worry, in all its forms, by reaching a general blanket decision that nothing life has to offer is worth the price of worry. With this decision will come poise, peace of mind, and calmness of thought, which will bring happiness.

YOU REALLY DO PICK UP ON
WHAT SOMEONE ELSE IS THINKING

A person whose mind is filled with fear not only destroys their own chances of intelligent action, but they then transmit these destructive vibrations to the minds of all who come into contact with them and also destroy their chances.

Even a dog or a horse knows when its master lacks courage. A dog or a horse will pick up the vibrations of fear thrown off by its master, and behave accordingly.

The vibrations of fear pass from one mind to another just as quickly and as surely as the sound of the human voice passes from the broadcasting station to the receiving set of a radio.

These thought impulses are not only damaging to others, but they embed themselves in the subconscious mind of the person releasing them, and there become a part of their character.

Mental telepathy is a reality. Thoughts pass from one mind to another voluntarily, whether or not this fact is recognized by either the person releasing the thoughts or the persons who pick up those thoughts.

One is never through with a thought merely by releasing it. When a thought is released it spreads in every direction, but it also plants itself in the subconscious of the person releasing it.

Hill uses the term *telepathy,* but his interpretation is his own, and it is quite different from the usual description of some kind of mystical or psychic phenomenon.

Hill's approach to telepathy is purely practical. The fact is that in real life we all get hunches and we all pick up "vibes" from some people. If we all have these experiences, and neither science nor psychology has yet to come up with an explanation of how these ideas get into our minds, Hill's theory of Infinite Intelligence provides a reasonable commonsense answer.

IT IS ALL UP TO YOU

You may control your own mind; you have the power to feed it whatever thought impulses you choose.

You are the master of your own earthly destiny just as surely as you have the power to control your own thoughts.

You may influence, direct, and eventually control your own environment, making your life what you want it to be.

Or you may neglect to exercise the privilege, thus casting yourself upon the broad sea of "circumstance," where you will be tossed hither and yon like a chip on the waves of the ocean.

THE DEVIL'S WORKSHOP: THE SEVENTH BASIC EVIL

In addition to the Six Basic Fears, there is another evil by which people suffer. For want of a better name, let us call this evil *susceptibility to negative influences.*

Without doubt, the most common weakness of all human beings is the habit of leaving their minds open to the negative influences of other people.

This weakness is all the more damaging because most people do not recognize that they are cursed by it. And many who do acknowledge it, neglect or refuse to correct the evil until it becomes an uncontrollable part of their daily habits.

HOW YOU CAN PROTECT YOURSELF AGAINST NEGATIVE INFLUENCES

You have absolute control over but one thing, and that is your thoughts. This is the most significant and inspiring of all facts known to man! It is the sole means by which you may control your own destiny. If you fail to control your own mind, you may be sure you will control nothing else. You were given willpower for this purpose.

Mind control is the result of self-discipline and habit. You either control your mind or it controls you. There is no halfway compromise.

The most practical of all methods for controlling the mind is the habit of keeping it busy with a definite purpose, backed by a definite plan.

ANYTHING YOUR MIND CAN CONCEIVE AND BELIEVE, YOU CAN ACHIEVE

In parting, I would remind you that "Life is a checkerboard and the player opposite you is time. If you hesitate before moving, or neglect to move promptly, your men will be wiped off the board by time. You are playing against a partner who will not tolerate indecision!"

Previously you may have had a logical excuse for not having forced Life to come through with whatever you asked, but that alibi is now obsolete, because you are in possession of the Master Key that unlocks the door to Life's bountiful riches.

The Master Key is intangible, but it is powerful! It is the privilege of creating, in your own mind, a burning desire for a definite form of riches. There is no penalty for the use of the Key, but there is a price you must pay if you do not use it.

That price is failure. There will be a reward of stupendous proportions if you put the Key to use. It is the satisfaction that comes to all who conquer self and force Life to pay whatever is asked.